AS204412

D0119983

Graham Ibbeson

Graham Ibbeson
The People's Sculptor

Bronze, Clay and Life

Graham Ibbeson & John Threlkeld

Wharncliffe Books

First published in Great Britain in 2011 by
Wharncliffe Books
an imprint of
Pen & Sword Books Ltd
47 Church Street
Barnsley
South Yorkshire
S70 2AS

ISBN 978 1 84884 571 8

A CIP catalogue record for this book is
available from the British Library.

Typeset in 11pt Minion by Mac Style, Beverley, East Yorkshire
Printed in China through Printworks Int.Ltd.

Pen & Sword Books Ltd incorporates the imprints of Pen & Sword Aviation, Pen &
Sword Maritime, Pen & Sword Military, Wharncliffe Local History, Pen & Sword
Select, Pen & Sword Military Classics, Leo Cooper, Seaforth Publishing and Frontline
Publishing.

For a complete list of Pen & Sword titles please contact
PEN & SWORD BOOKS LIMITED
47 Church Street, Barnsley, South Yorkshire, S70 2AS, England

Contents

Foreword

It is virtually impossible to speak the words 'Graham Ibbeson' without committing the biggest name-dropping crime of the century. Eric Morecambe, Cary Grant, Laurel & Hardy, Fred Trueman, William Webb Ellis, Dickie Bird, Les Dawson, the list goes on and on.

Not only has he sculpted these famous folk, his works have been unveiled by some pretty impressive celebrities. Oh, and that includes Her Majesty the Queen! Is there anyone of public notability that hasn't come into contact with, or under the x-ray eyes and swashbuckling scalpel of what some (me included) believe to be one of Britain's greatest figurative sculptors?

His extensive works have taught me that when courage, conviction, wisdom and wit, extraordinary observation and a blank refusal to swallow propaganda come together, the miraculous occurs.

Just take a look at the tallest freestanding sculpture in Nottinghamshire. A twice life-size modern miner, on top of a 12-foot lamp containing a life-size figure of an old miner wearing a flat cap, stripped to the waist and shovelling coal. No sentiment, no romance, just honest gritty pride, depicting nothing short of a modern day warrior carrying out his duty of keeping the fires burning and the lights switched on.

In his public bronze the Spirit of Jarrow depicting two protestors, a mother and baby, two small children plus a mongrel dog (the marchers' mascot), we are given a poignant reminder that in our current turbulent economic climate the pendulum of unemployment still swings, some seventy-four years after these marchers took their 12,000 signatures, protesting the closure of Tyneside shipyards, to 10 Downing Street.

These public commissions are undoubtedly tremendous achievements for Ibbeson and stand as testament to his brilliant ability to tell it as it is. But, it's the uniquely personal and poignant creations of Ibbeson's own imagination that interest me the most. These pieces have been in considerable demand in recent years, not least because his perspective misses nothing. The sanguine with the sinister, the tender with the torment, sit side by side buckled into the brow of his characters who are all 'out and proud', occupying their rightful place on the plinths of prestigious galleries and museums around the world, boastful of their lineage and petulant to any suggestion that only the serious get taken seriously.

Just reading the titles, Compact Colin, Freddy Neptune, North Sea Nippers, Down To Earth, Really Fished Off and Wife On The Ocean Wave, spark the imagination and tickle the laughing tackle, before viewing the work itself pushes you way beyond humour, into questioning just what it is that lies behind these seemingly simple clichés. Visiting an Ibbeson exhibition can be a rather surreal experience. Nothing much prepares you for the sheer eccentricity of it all. It's a bit like stepping onto the set of *The City of Lost Children*, the movie by acclaimed director Jean-Pierre Jeunet, in which a mad scientist kidnaps children so as to steal their dreams. Just as Jeunet plays tricks with the audience's expectations, Ibbeson's sculptures demand many viewings if we are to find out what on earth's really going on. He is one of the those rare artists who can make me stare in wonder, laugh my socks off, shed a tear and, on occasion, do all at the same time.

The majority of Ibbeson's non-commissioned works appear super animated and very photogenic. It may be only a matter of time before Compact Colin or Freddy Neptune make it into the pages of a graphic novel or onto the cutting room floor.

Over our long term working relationship I have gained much respect for Graham Ibbeson. I am honoured to have been privy to some unique insights into the extraordinary talent of this ordinary 'Barnsley bloke' and I am delighted that this book now affords the public at large some of the same.

Phil Tregoning of Tregoning Fine Art, Derby

Introduction

It's really odd picking over my life as a sculptor. I have grown old and my statues are suspended in time, with their sulks and quirky smiles. They seem to be frozen in a world that has spun into a technological frenzy. Looking back on some of the pieces I can remember why I came up with the concept of each work but cannot remember sculpting it. The statement was more important than the process of making the statement. Over forty years I have produced a natural family and have made 'families' of sculptures as well.

This book maps out my life. It focuses on my childhood and teenage years and examines my work, humour and skills and burrows into the artistic nooks and crannies in my mind.

I would like to thank my friends, family and colleagues for their support and encouragement on this forty-year trek through the arts and in particular my wife, Carol, and children, Faye, Emma and Max, who have trod the road with me. I would also like to thank Brian Elliott, the commissioning editor, whose skills have enabled us to compile the biography. Lastly I would like to give a special thanks to John Threlkeld who encouraged me to be open about my life, and documented it with his own distinctive prose and humour; our friendship is still intact (thank goodness) after many months of working on this book.

Graham Ibbeson 2011

Chapter 1

Early Days

The 18-stone man in overalls was carrying a crowbar and mallet and looked more like a burglar in search of swag than a VIP poised to enjoy the pomp and celebration of a Royal visit. Graham Ibbeson, the sculptor, was walking along the seafront at Morecambe on route to examine his statue of one of Britain's much loved comedians, Eric Morecambe. It was 6am on 23 July 1999, and within a few hours Her Majesty the Queen would unveil the work amid all the pageantry and show that the Lancashire resort could muster. The security barriers had been erected, the tourists were beginning to arrive and the union flags and bunting added colour to the seafront. Graham, preparing to give the statue a once over before the big event, used the crowbar and mallet to prise away the wooden boards which had encased the figure for several weeks.

The artist was startled by what he saw, then paused and listened in case the spirit of the comedian was chuckling in a quiet corner. The bronze sculpture had changed colour – from brown to green. A kind of micro climate inside the large wooden 'box' had larked around with the metal to create a colourful reaction. It was a classic last minute crisis – it had happened at least once before at a ceremony in Derbyshire where the figure turned blue – and as the clock ticked away and the streets fizzed with expectation he had to apply some serious elbow grease to remove the green stain.

Once the job was done and dusted he walked back to the B and B, designer stubble and all, and past the thickets of police officers and secret service men who had earlier given his crowbar a quizzical look when he showed them his pass to get through the security line. Few people on or near the seafront realised that this was the man broadcaster Sir Robin Day would describe as the genius behind the statue.

As he strolled in the sunshine, Graham was not thinking of how to attain perfection in art or mulling over aspects of his ancient craft – he was wondering what would have happened if Eric's green rash had been there when Her Majesty had removed the wraps. It was an almost farcical start to the day but, then, Eric Morecambe and Graham are what madcap humour are all about even on a right Royal occasion.

By the time Her Majesty the Queen had arrived from a function in Lancaster thousands of waiting spectators were in a carnival mood and the press photographers,

Her Majesty the Queen unveils the Eric Morecambe statue. *Morecambe Visitor*

Graham (third right) next to the Queen. *Morecambe Visitor*

'Eric in the clay'. Graham did not realise at the time that holidaymakers would became so enamoured by this statue that years later they would form a statue appreciation society. *Ibbeson Collection*

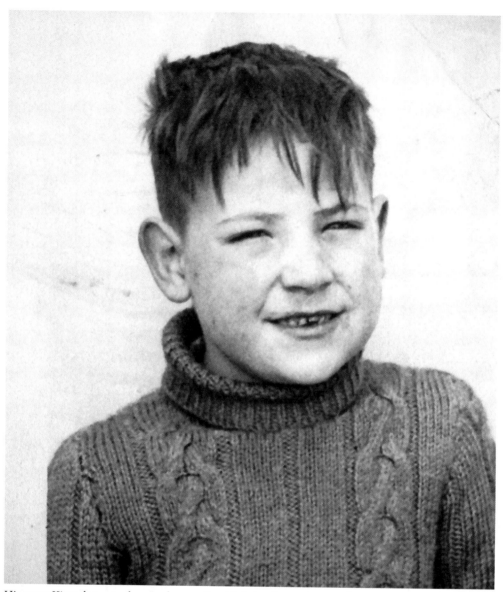

His mum Kitty always took care when parting his hair when young. At the age of six, however, he used the scissors at school to give himself a brave new look before the photographer arrived. His mother was not amused. *Ibbeson Family Archive*

in Graham's words, 'were hanging from the lamp-posts'. But amid the excitement there was a brief scene which produced a wry thought. The Queen approached the statue from behind and below and had to walk up a few stone steps. Anyone standing in front of Eric, with the sea as a backdrop, would have seen her head and then body gradually coming into view, almost like one of the star guests as they walked up the grand stairway

This photograph depicts a beaming – and much smarter – Graham in the fields leading to Three Nooks Lane. The Lane was part of the 'secret' route from his home to the neighbouring village of Cudworth where both sets of grandparents, most of his relatives and his secondary school pals lived.

That's where Cousin Paul also lived. 'He was the nearest thing to a brother I had. He was my younger victim of torment (as in his George and Eric characters) and in adult life an intelligent and creative friend (he is now a teacher and writer).' *Ibbeson Family Archive*

His Dad and Mum (front left and back left) and his maternal grandparents, Ada and Joe, at the back door of his grandparents' home in Pontefract Road, Cudworth. The photograph was probably taken before his parents were married in 1950. *Ibbeson Family Archive*

'George and Eric at the barbers'. It was inspired by Graham's hair-cutting incident. *Freddy Neptune Limited*

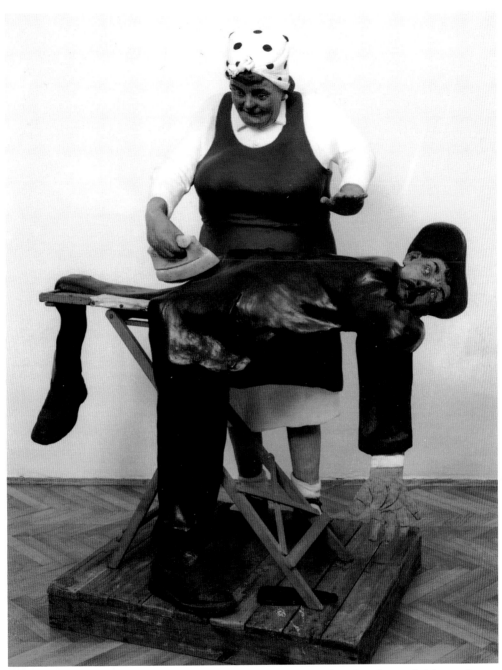

Graham's childhood memories helped to forge his outlook on life and on his work. This sculpture, 'Woman Flattens Husband', was prompted by an incident involving his maternal grandparents. The ironing board was bought by Carol in the Second-Hand Market because she thought it could be used in the course of his work. It languished in his studio for several years. One night he was walking home from the pub when a mate told him: 'The wife will flatten you when you get home.' That comment triggered his inventiveness. *The Nicholas Treadwell Gallery*

Before working at Slazenger's his grandfather was employed on the surface at a pit and he is pictured (first left) on a lathe. *Ibbeson Family Archive*

Graham says he was his grandparents' favourite grandchild. Ada cradles Graham while two unidentified children look on. *Ibbeson Family Archive*

Graham's paternal grandparents. Left to right: Grandfather Len, Uncle Stan on the wall, Grandmother Elsie and Graham's father, Granville. Len was an engineer at the Slazenger's factory in Barnsley. Every day he rode his bike from his home in Cudworth to Barnsley and back. After he retired he was asked to return to work for a while to help his successor. On his last day he returned home on the bus, alighted and had a heart attack. He died days later in hospital and never had the chance to enjoy his retirement. *Ibbeson Family Archive*

situated behind the comedy duo on the *Morecambe and Wise Show*. She greeted Graham, now attired in a smart suit and without the stubble, with a smile and 'hello' and went on to meet the assembled VIPs before the unveiling.

As soon as the ceremony was over a wave of applause slapped against the sea front and Prince Philip shouted: 'What do you think of it so far?' The spectators roared back in unison with the comedian's catch word: 'Rubbish!' Prince Philip leaned over towards Graham and smiled: 'Only jesting, lad.' At that point Graham, who is unbelievably nervous before an unveiling, relaxed and the shock at seeing Eric's unplanned green splurge receded.

From the day of the unveiling the statue was destined to become a significant tourist attraction. The story and photographs were sprawled across the pages of the following morning's newspapers. It had struck a nostalgic chord with a nation of Eric Morecambe fans. In the subsequent year the car park revenues in Morecambe increased by £1 million as families came to be photographed with the legendary comedian performing his Sunshine Dance. So thankful were the traders in the resort they gave Graham the official title of Ambassador to Morecambe and Lancaster. The procession of holidaymakers has been continuous over eleven years, though 2010 has seen a new development as the statue has taken on a 'life' of its own: an Eric Morecambe Statue Appreciation Society has been formed with more than 300 members and Graham is thinking of creating miniature 'Erics' in Morecambe rock.

Graham, now an acclaimed sculptor, acknowledges the unveiling brought sunshine into his life and that he has come a long way from the pits and the grey council estates of his childhood in Barnsley. It has been a journey of discovery. He has turned his back on what would have been a familiar job, married at the age of seventeen when he and Carol 'were still kids' and was a student at the prestigious Royal College of Art while having a family to support. His subsequent success – his work has been sold all over the world – has not been bad for a lad who left school at the age of fifteen without any qualifications.

He was born on 13 August 1951. It was the year of The Festival of Britain, London smogs and the last vestiges of rationing and post war austerity. When he was three or four years old the family moved from a flat above a doctor's surgery into a new pit house at Shafton, near Barnsley, in the heart of the Yorkshire coalfield. Graham said: 'We lived on the edge of fields but you could see and smell the pit.'

The pits dominated life both underground and on the surface. The sounds of mining were always audible – even in the fields. Three Nooks Lane was nearby. It was part of the route the family took to visit grandparents, relatives and friends in the neighbouring village of Cudworth. Graham said: 'The "fields' way" took us on a route from our house through two huge fields, past a rubbish tip and on to Three Nooks Lane, past the water

'The miner' commissioned by the former Yorkshire mining village of South Kirkby. Graham has captured the essence of a face worker in this work. He has skilfully emphasised the broad back of a miner. It was so important to miners to keep their backs in top condition. Sixty years ago lotions and creams were used to ease aches and pains and wives made thick woollen belts to support the lower regions of the back.

Once a miner had a weakened back his job was in jeopardy because he would not be able to produce enough coal to meet productivity levels on which his wages were based. In the early twentieth century many miners believed that washing weakened the back and therefore during the working week went to bed with their backs covered in coal dust. Graham is seen here with the Town Clerk. *Ibbeson Collection*

An evocative picture from the days of mining. His father (right) is with a colleague, probably a pit deputy (foreman). The scene, a wonderful piece of social history, was photographed outside New Monckton No 1 Colliery in 1954. The pit had baths for the men but on the left there is a miner with coal dust on his face. Some miners went home to bathe even after the installation of pithead baths because they needed privacy.

The family had strong connections with the industry. According to the death certificate his great, great grandmother, Sarah Ibbeson, died 'at the Main Colliery, Wombwell', in 1871. At that time women were employed on the surface at pits and she may have died while working there. But certificates in those days were sometimes inaccurate and there is a chance she was a housewife who passed away in one of the houses in the pit yard or in one of the nearby rows of miners' homes. *Ibbeson Family Archive*

tower and into the village. As children my sister, Gail, and I thought of it as the family's secret route from our house. We were too small to see the pit stacks of Monckton or notice the tip before you got to the lane.'

In the fields they could hear the creaking of the large pit buckets which were suspended from the overhead cables and which carried and deposited waste from the underground workings onto spoil heaps just over the hill. 'In fact, the noise of the buckets was an ever present background noise of my early childhood, rumbling and creaking. The noise was part of the fabric of the estate, like the smell of the spoil heaps and of the green fields and the look of the pebble-dashed Wimpey (Coal Board) houses. In late childhood this path gave me my own space, a time to think and contemplate the world. Since then I have walked this path many times with my children on my shoulders, the same path my dad trod with me on his.'

The family had a strong mining background. His father, Kenneth Granville Ibbeson, worked at Monckton Colliery and his maternal grandfather, Joseph Patrick Thwaites, a Geordie, at Grimethorpe Colliery, then one of the largest in the Barnsley coalfield. Their way of life – like most miners they were proud of their heightened physical prowess – has helped to sharpen his artistic work. While nationalisation in 1947 had ushered in a new era in mining, the underground worker in the 1950s still had a job which demanded strength. As a writer said many years ago miners were like hammered statues of iron under a coating of coal dust and this image has been used by Graham in a series of mining memorials and statues over the last twenty years. His bronze statue commissioned by the former mining village of South Kirkby, near Hemsworth, West Yorkshire, in 2005, captured the physical essence and presence of a miner as he 'fights' a wall of coal with his pick. Graham said: 'His back is wider than in real life and ripples with muscle. The figure is an exaggeration but I think I have taken the conventional image of a miner a step further. I was destined to do that statue. My father had worked at Riddings Colliery, part of South Kirkby pit, and I had lived a couple of villages away from South Kirkby.' Feeling a sense of awe when recalling those miners, particularly his father who had formidable strength in his arms and legs, he said: 'He worked in small spaces underground and as a result could rest on his haunches. I have seen him resting like that while smoking at a bus stop; I do not know how he managed that physically demanding stance for so long.'

Their work may have hardened muscles but miners' lungs were prematurely withered by the dust in the atmosphere in the mine workings: in the days before nationalisation the dust could be so dense as to neutralize the beam from a lamp. Graham, while sitting in the house, knew when his father was walking up the street by his distinctive and persistent cough.

His maternal grandfather and grandmother had blistering and memorable battles. His grandmother, Ada, was small and fiery. Overwrought and intoxicated, his grandfather arrived home late one Sunday and threw his meal onto the coal fire, declaring that it was too cold to eat. On the following Sunday, arriving home on time, he settled down to enjoy his roast beef and Yorkshire pudding but his wife was too quick, grabbed the plate and hurled the food into the burning coal. He went into a black rage and Ada, now exhibiting all her coiled and hidden fury, retaliated by throwing a sharpened fork which arrowed its way through the air and speared his forehead. The four tines on the fork drew flecks of blood and left behind miniscule puncture marks. The following day he went to work as usual and while underground the ever present coal dust 'sealed' the cuts: for the rest of his life he had the blue marks on his forehead, a constant reminder of the day when his wife had wildly demonstrated she was not to be put on.

Such marks or scars were an occupational hazard. All miners had them, mainly on their backs where the coal dust found its way into small cuts or abrasions before they had healed; but the majority could not blame the wife for their minor disfigurements – they worked in confined spaces and their backs were often inches away from the jagged pieces of rock and coal in the seam. The marks were seen as 'badges of courage' by young men in the early twentieth century, 'Coal Board tattoos' to modern miners. It was said that old miners, who believed coal contained healthy properties, rubbed the dust into their cuts to facilitate healing.

Meanwhile, his grandparents' stories and antics incubated and loitered in his mind for years before being reshaped into amusing episodes and woven into his work: in one of his pieces a wife in an apron relishes ironing flat her fearful husband on the ironing board, an act of retribution for his dalliance in the pub. To Graham the electric iron was a much more efficient and scary weapon than a fork.

His grandfather loved devilment, camaraderie and humour. 'The work was hard but the men got on well together and they had a lot of laughs,' said Graham. 'I have tried to persuade people to look at life through laughter.' Miners used humour to help cope with the perverse and primitive working conditions underground. That jocularity spilled over into their social life. On a New Year's Eve the revellers went home after a session in the pub. 'My grandfather was sat under the table; he did not like parties and did not want to be the centre of attention. But he did enjoy being an instigator.' The partygoers were playing a game, at the end of which his grandfather's unfortunate mate Frank Hardman had to forfeit a prized possession, a lone hair on his chest known as 'Wally'. The miners lathered his chest, a razor was produced and 'Wally' was removed with a flick of the fingers and a surfeit of humour. It was pure theatre, the best party the world had ever known, a youthful Graham concluded as he sat in the warm room and listened

His mum as a schoolgirl in 1942. Kitty, who was born in the North East, became a nurse and a member of the Labour Party in the Barnsley area. She married at the age of twenty, his dad was twenty-one. *Ibbeson Family Archive*

His father's picture appeared in Coal News when he produced this miniature domestic scene, having made all the fixtures and furniture himself. He started this kind of work after Graham studied at college.

His father's generation had all kinds of hidden skills. His father was adept at repairing radios and lawnmowers. Graham said: 'People brought things to our house to be repaired when I was young. In the old days families kept things going as long as possible. The consumer society had not yet arrived. Years later I felt guilty when I bought a new flat screen television on the grounds I could not repair the old one.' *Coal News*

to the comradely chatter as the snow drifted outside the window. Memories of the party remained with him for years, as did his recollections of his grandfather's masterly use of homespun merriment and the swirl of childhood images such as tin baths, dustbin lids, flat caps and catapults, which have been used to great effect in his work.

They never said it but Graham knew he was the favoured grandchild of his maternal grandparents and the feeling was mutual. 'Maybe it was because I was the first born. I'd like to think that my grandmother saw some of her husband's traits in me and my grandfather saw a fellow conspirator. We visited them at least three times a week (my father seldom came) and Gail, my younger sister, and I loved it. At home we had to tip-toe around the house ("You'll wake your dad up"; he always seemed to be on nights). At our grandparents' home we could run riot. I was thirteen when they took me on holiday to Blackpool; we were in the street when my grandfather complained of chest pains and of feeling unwell. A slight heart attack was diagnosed by a doctor back at the B and B and the holiday was cut short. 'He never worked at Grimey pit again and he was bored silly. He would wait at the window and beam when he saw us coming around the corner in anticipation of aggravating his grandchildren and daughter. My mother stormed out on numerous occasions when the tormenting got too much, vowing never to return. We all knew it was an idle threat, especially my grandfather.'

On a day never to be forgotten, Graham, having been thrown out of the house by his father after an acrimonious row, was at his grandparents' house. It had a been a traumatic and nightmarish day – he had walked without shoes for several miles, languishing only at his favourite spot, Three Nooks Lane – but what happened next left him slipping helplessly into a crisis which may have been one of the reasons why he moved from Barnsley. It happened so abruptly. His hot tempered grandmother, who had been wielding the carving knife around like a sword and threatening revenge on Graham's father for ejecting Graham, was calming down. 'Gail was dancing in an amateur production that evening. My grandparents were getting ready to go along when my grandfather stumbled, shouted "Ada" and fell. I tried mouth-to-mouth resuscitation but it was too late and he died in my arms. I was sixteen, Gail was thirteen.'

Earlier, at school, there had been little to indicate he would become an artist. However, there was one incident which he enjoys recalling. His first lesson in the subject had that zany touch which became the hallmark of his work. He was a pupil at Shafton Infants' School and one afternoon the teacher gave the children a stern warning about the foolishness of nasal exploration, a practice which was becoming popular in the classroom. In other words they were banned from shoving pieces of crayon up their noses. Graham, as usual, disobeyed orders and to his horror his piece would not budge in his nostril, at which point the thought blazed across his mind he was going to die. The doctor burst into laughter as he came to the rescue and removed the obstruction using a pair of tweezers. Graham admits he could be a nuisance and at one point his mother was told in no uncertain terms that he had to stop using the nickname Mrs Dripping when referring to a teacher, Mrs Tipping.

While at infants and junior school he kept Dr Tobin busy and amused. There was a small disused quarry, a playground for the estate, where a 'follow my leader' game nearly ended in tragedy. He was six years old, smaller than the other children, and did not quite make it while jumping over a rusty pram.

'I remember looking at my knee and seeing all this yellow stuff hanging out; my mother's face went the same colour when she saw the injury. I was dragged through the fields with my three-year-old sister to Dr Tobin's surgery in the next village where I was given three stitches. I did not heed the doctor or my mother's advice not to "lake" (play) out for a week or so, and I bust the stitches in a matter of days, having to receive another five. A wide scar adorns my right knee today.'

Later that year he broke his left arm when running through one of Farmer Nunny's fields. At least his vulnerability to injury ('I was not so much accident prone as boisterous') continued to amuse the doctor who had earlier removed the crayon from his nose and who had inserted the stitches in his knee. 'When I told the doctor I had done it falling over a cabbage he laughed; even at six I thought he was not taking my pain seriously. I broke it again less than a year later when larking about in the school playground: no wonder I enjoy sculpting in plaster.'

At about the age of nine the family moved to a council house farther up the village. Like most miners his dad wanted to get out of the pit to find another job – for working underground had no redeeming features. That move to a council property was seen as the first step to freedom; unfortunately he never achieved his goal and he worked at the mine until he accepted redundancy after the miners' strike. The playground was a quadrangle in the middle of the estate. One day childhood imaginations were running wild and Graham, fencing in the best traditions of a French musketeer, rapped his opponent's knuckles with his rapier-like stick. Unlike a musketeer, Graham ran like hell and his adversary, in a rage, hurled an iron rod which speared its way through the air like his grandmother's quivering fork and pierced the top of his right arm a couple of inches from a lung.

For a few moments the honour of France was forgotten and a band of cowboys pursued by Red Indians galloped through his thoughts. He grimaced, Hollywood-style, and plucked the rod from his arm like a cowboy pulling an Apache arrow out of a shoulder as the Indians raided the wagon train. Then the pain shrieked through his body and mind. 'I was no John Wayne. I shook the estate with my screams on the way back to my mam.' He was crying and shouting: 'I am dead, I am dead...' as he sped past his sister who was playing outside. Gail started to weep, walked away and said to a friend: 'Graham is dead, he's dead.' But the friend, surprised, replied: 'He's not dead; I have just seen him running home.'

At secondary school art lessons, like gardening and sport, were seen as a relief from academic studies. He would like to say that he was inspired to become an artist from an early age, 'but there was no lighting of the blue touch paper of creativity'. Whereas other boys were preoccupied with how toys and machines worked, Graham was concerned about how they looked. But in the annual report in his third year his art teacher wrote that infamous cliché, "could do better". In his final year things started to change.

In 1966 he was preparing to leave the Cudworth Secondary Modern School and the careers officer arrived to help pupils find a job. His mother, Kitty, who did not want him to work down a pit like his father and grandfather, was there to give him support, though she did not know Graham had already lined up an interview for a job at the National Coal Board workshops on his doorstep at Shafton. During the interview with the careers officer a prefect walked into the room and asked him to go to the school hall where the annual presentation of trophies was taking place. To his surprise he was presented with the trophy for having made the most progress in art during the year. He was exuberant but did not show it – Gail, known as 'Ar Ugly' (she isn't ugly but Graham likes the word), who was in the assembly, said he looked so cool. On returning to the room with the large silver plated trophy and a new sense of pride, he said: 'What do you think of this, Mam?' His joy, however, turned to disappointment: the careers officer looked at his shoulders (he had been 5 ft 11 inches at the age of twelve) and asked: 'Would you like to be a farm labourer?'

Graham, now concentrating on art rather than a job down on the farm, was impressed by Vincent Van Gogh. He submitted a portrait of him to a small exhibition at a summer gala shortly after leaving school. It was a sunny day on 30 July 1966, the gala was well organised, there were plenty of attractions and his painting in the marquee almost begged for public recognition. Graham was conspicuously absent. Not many other people bothered to turn up either, for the nation was jubilantly preoccupied with that jamboree known as the World Cup. Graham, like millions of others, was watching on television England beat Germany 4-2 in front of 98,000 fans at Wembley while his painting languished at the gala. By tea time the Germans knew it was all over and Vincent Van Gogh's protégé realised it was all over as far as his painting was concerned. 'I have often heard artists talk about the first time they saw their framed picture on the wall, saying they were overcome by what I call emulsion, but not me. I never went back to collect my masterpiece.'

The smell of grease mixed with coal dust pervaded the workshops where he became an apprentice electrician at the age of fifteen. It was a place where most things were familiar,

Mum, Graham and Gail. *Ibbeson Family Archive*

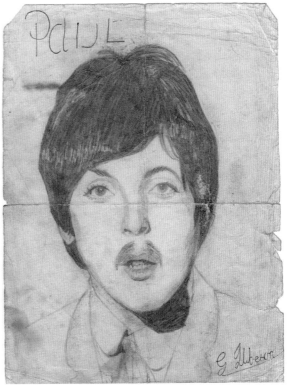

An example of Graham's drawing skills when he was a young teenager – Beatle Paul. *Ibbeson Collection*

like the people, humour and sounds, but he was unhappy. 'They got us doing anything. Skips which were to be filled with coal and old materials were first painted white, and what was the point of that?' Graham and his pals were the first apprentices to be taken on at the workshops where colliery machinery was repaired and maintained, and he believes management did not know what to do with the lads, hence the unusual tasks they were given. It did not take him long to come to a critical realisation – he had to move on.

Graham's opportunity to change course came when his mother's friend, Mrs Mavis Taff, a former teacher, took him to Barnsley Art School. His aim was to spend three years there, after which he would go to university or polytechnic. His parents were very supportive and encouraged him. In 1967 he started on a fine art course, exchanging the odour of grease and oil at the workshops for the smell of oil paints. 'I was more interested in the concept of becoming an artist rather than being an artist. It was going to be one big party; we all wanted to be like John Lennon and pull women.

'I still remember in great detail the walk from Barnsley Bus Station to the art school with the anticipation of a future full of creative expression; I had my portfolio under my arm and a small rucksack full of artist's materials. I was going to be forever young and I did not envisage a future carving a career out of making sculptures.

'I still live quite close to the local art college and watch the students walking to and fro. Okay their clothes are still expressive, so are their hairstyles and even their gait. However, the only thing that differentiates an art student from the rest of the pack is the black portfolios they carry. In the 1960s art students stood out from their fellow students. It was not an education; it was a way of life.'

The tutor, on his first day out of college, was about four years older than Graham. He asked the students to put their pencils on the desks. 'Now break them,' said the tutor. 'From now on you will use your creativity.' The students had to use all kinds of bizarre substitutes including twigs dipped in ink. Graham added later: 'He wanted us to think in another way. We had to learn to improvise and that's what I am doing today.'

At that time Graham was not prepared to handle the hard work – his attitude changed at college – and, at any rate, adventure and the beach beckoned. On a more serious note he wanted to escape from the pit village and Barnsley. In those days the inward looking mining communities were beginning to creak as the older pits closed and young people with restless ambition moved on.

The UK underwent an exciting social revolution in the 1960s and the would-be sculptor turned his back on the dour villages and the drudgery of an old way of life. In a way, by getting out of the mining industry, he had realised an ambition his father had found so infuriatingly elusive. That cannot be construed as criticism of his father: he had been a member of a working- class generation which had far fewer opportunities for advancement.

Chapter 2

Romance and a New World

During the summer holidays Graham, aged sixteen, fell in love with a girl in The Star Cafe and his life moved dramatically in another direction. He and a mate had gone to work in the cafe in Mablethorpe, the Lincolnshire resort. A beautiful blonde and leggy girl walked in with her pal and asked for fish, chips and peas. That was enough to charm and then disarm Graham who was wiping tables and after some innocent flirtation he teamed up with Carol Greenwood, who was on holiday, and his pal with her friend. When Carol returned home to Ripley in Derbyshire he went to see her. On the first day he learned that the town's likeable characters were similar to the ones back home. While walking down the street the couple spotted a little man who was eating chips and who kept smiling at Carol. Who was he? Nothing was said. Graham thought he must be the local eccentric or drunk and dismissed him from his mind. That night the visitor from Barnsley slept on the couch and the following morning the little stranger walked downstairs still smiling, it was Carol's father, Charlie, who became one of Graham's instant mates.

Life in Ripley could be given a shot of mental caffeine by instigating the occasional practical joke. It was Carol who spoilt her father's would-be stint in the pub by unstitching his going out suit; he was on the point of leaving the house when the jacket and trousers fell apart like one of Laurel and Hardy's rickety model T-Fords, 'ending up looking like a dress'. Graham fell apart on hearing the story and Charlie followed his daughter and Graham's dad into becoming models for his future sculptures, all of whom would be modelled in clay. Then their likenesses were fashioned into fibreglass or bronze and sent all over Europe and the USA for the benefit of posterity. Charlie, the little miner, one of seventeen siblings, had joined the Army in his youth to ensure he had a square meal, later becoming a Desert Rat in the war. Graham says he had 'the smile of a drinker, the smile of a warm person' and everyone of his generation in Ripley greeted him with the equally warm: 'Hey up, Charlie, how are you?' In the future he attained minor celebrity status hundreds of miles from the rolling Derbyshire hills when one of the statues based on him was seen by millions on television in Holland – but that's another story.

The holiday romance turned serious and flourished and within nine months at Whitsuntide, 1969, they were married, though they stressed it was not a shotgun wedding. More than forty years on the marriage is still intact and the family is as strong as ever.

Carol on holiday in Blackpool in 1968. *Ibbeson Family Archive*

Graham with Sammy the dog in High Street, Shafton, before his marriage. He is seen wearing his hat back to front… no dedicated follower of fashion. *Ibbeson Family Archive*

From 1969 Graham did a variety of jobs in the Ripley area including working at Thornton's sweet factory at Belper where the bosses believed his artistic background would help him to acquire the skills to adorn Easter eggs with sugary flowers. He was transferred to the hard-boiled sweet room and smelt of peppermint for years, 'which was better than some of the smells coming off my colleagues'. His mother-in-law, Mabel, sensing his unease with his work, said: 'He'll be all right when he does something he wants to do and settles down.' They were wise words.

His artistic feet were itching again and he enrolled at Chesterfield Art School, ignoring the advice of his paternal grandfather who had said art was okay but was not a proper job. It was a daunting prospect since he had a mortgage and daughter, Faye, born in 1970, was a year old. 'I was twentyish and was accepted on a foundation course; I was studying for GCE 'O' levels and Carol continued to work. I worked very hard and I was conscious that I came from a working class background and that I was educationally inadequate. I worked part-time doing anything and studied on the bus going to and coming from the college.'

The couple were married at Brierley, near Barnsley, Register Office in 1969 (it was not a shotgun wedding). The guests were few and after the service a table was booked at the Co-operative restaurant in Barnsley. Then the couple caught the coach for the honeymoon in Blackpool. There was a daily service to and from the resort and the couple chose Blackpool so they could return home before the end of the week if necessary. Money was scarce. Contrast that wedding with their son Max's 'do' several years ago. He was married at the former home of the Wentworth family at Wentworth Castle, Stainborough; the hire of the wedding cars and the cost of the flowers came to £2,000 and the couple honeymooned in the Maldives. *Ibbeson Family Archive*

He was still awaiting the results of his exams when he was accepted at Leicester Polytechnic on the grounds of what the tutors said was his 'outstanding artistic ability'. 'The interview at Leicester was horrendous; I was so nervous that sweat marked some of the drawings I had with me. I was scared I would have to go back and find a job like welding which I had done before. This feeling that it couldn't last haunted me for years, but I kept going because my wife and daughter had made sacrifices so that I could go to college.'

Graham became the unexpected hero on the fine art course at Leicester Polytechnic. A lecturer asked the class: 'Could you tell me what is Art?' There was no answer from the students, so he tried again and focused on Graham, asking him the same question. His

Graham and Carol on honeymoon and they haven't a care in the world. The couple stayed at a boarding house, the owners of which kept peering at Carol's wedding ring because the newlyweds looked so young. *Ibbeson Family Archive*

reply: 'No; I bloody can't give you an answer, I have no idea.' The lecturer smiled and said: 'That is the correct answer particularly at this stage of your career.' The faces of the other students lit with admiration. Important as the course was, Graham was stifled and disaffection set in. The college wanted formal sculptures and this free spirit who knew what he wanted rebelled. He was also missing Carol and Faye, prompting him to get a transfer nearer home to Nottingham Polytechnic where there was more space for what was becoming finely crafted work. A studio was shared with John Shippey, who went into films, and Tim Stead, who later became a bespoke furniture maker.

Graham was the only person in his year doing figurative sculpture and specialised in life-sized figures and dabbled in garden gnomes which may seem a peculiar choice for an ambitious sculptor; but it was all part of the learning process. His only experience of sculptures had been the austere figure of a soldier on the local war memorial back home and the gnomes which were springing up in gardens all over the country. He immersed himself in making and then fretting over his new pals, a bunch of skilfully conceived but mean-looking gnomes who seemed to scrutinise onlookers from deep sockets. A scaled-down thatched cottage was built to make them cosily secure and bespoke furniture added as if the gnomes wished to impress the neighbours: the whole scene had the captivating quality of a Walt Disney film. He made clothes, knives and forks for them and manicured turf was laid in the studio. At the time he did not realise he was starting an unusual trend which has reappeared throughout his career – an alternative family – but more about that later.

After that project he progressed to models of dwarfs, but that vein of creativity petered out and he went to the other extreme, a larger-than-life horse. Like the gnomes' pastoral paradise, the horse grew and grew, becoming a 15ft-high plaster model which soon occupied a vast amount of space in the studio. Scaffolding was erected around this equestrian beauty, eliciting the curiosity of visitors, and he continued to work on it for a year only to come to the conclusion the scale was too ambitious. The horse was broken up before completion and a valuable lesson was absorbed. 'Even now, after forty years in the arts, I would keep away from tackling such a large project.'

It's his opinion that he obtained a first class honours degree at Nottingham Polytechnic in 1975 for being daft. Did the degree prove anything? 'It helped to develop my work and meet like-minded people.' Now he had options – studying for another degree, moving into teaching or becoming an artist. Teacher-training was chosen on the grounds he had to support Carol and two children, his second daughter, Emma, having been born in 1974. At the interview he was asked: 'Why do you want to become a teacher?' His reply: 'I want to subsidise my art work.' It was not the right answer: he was the only person from the college who applied to study on a teacher training course that year who did not get a place. Then he was selected to study at the Royal College of Art, together with

John Shippey, who was accepted by the Film School at the College. The interview was conducted as London sweltered in flaming June. The heat got to Graham, he sweated profusely and the old anxiety resurfaced: he thought the interview was a shambles. But the College staff knew better and the Marquis of Queensbury, a professor of ceramics, and Sir Eduardo Paolozzi, one of the few British artists who came to international prominence soon after the Second World War, were impressed. 'I thought I had been atrocious but they loved my work and loved my attitude to work.'

The family moved into a flat off Fulham Road in August 1975, where they stayed for three years. He was on a ceramics course in the main building next to the Albert Hall. Unfortunately the sculpture school was 500 yards away, so tantalisingly close, and every day he walked past the entrance. It was time for another critical realisation and his passion for his craft overwhelmed any loyalty to the ceramics course. After a brief spell on the course he walked mercurially into the sculpture school and announced to an astonished Professor Bernard Meadows that he wanted to make a sculpture of a 40-seater bus going to the seaside. Changing his mind, Graham drew on another childhood memory – his father had had a push bike and sidecar – and created a motor-cycle and side-car ridden by a naked and exuberant woman. A dog running after the sidecar was added to the work, then a running man and finally a girl looking on. It was a brilliantly enigmatic image which radiated fun. Professor Meadows, bemused by the sudden appearance of the lady and the motorbike, rubbed his chin and asked: 'I thought you were doing a bust?' 'No,' replied an equally astonished Graham, 'I said a bus.' The grey-haired professor, unversed in the nuances of the Yorkshire accent, stroked his chin again and walked away. The work on the sculpture continued at a frenetic pace as he pressed his aim to get into the school; the poor professor, finally coerced into submission, shouted: 'Stop, stop, I'll give you your transfer.' Graham went into the ceramics school through the front door and into the sculpture school through the back door.

Attached to the college was a foundry specialising in bronze. The founder was Tissa Ranasinge, from Sri Lanka, a sculptor artist who taught him more about the craft than some members of the teaching staff. Graham called him 'Dad', reviving a custom from the mining days when young miners referred to an older workmate as 'Dad'. The word did attract some funny looks when they both went for a drink after a hard day in the foundry where Graham worked part-time as a labourer to supplement his grant. One of the perks of the job was that he learned the trade and there was a sense of exhilaration when he cast his first work in bronze. But outside the foundry, on the grounds of expense, he had to remain with fibre-glass.

Professor Meadows, who had been a personal assistant to Henry Moore, was a mentor, introducing him to his first gallery in Knightsbridge, and in 1976 he had his first exhibition of small bronzes and drawings there and the drawings were sold. By 1977 he was exhibiting at the Nicholas Treadwell Gallery in the West End. Despite the change in his circumstances, and now living in a world far removed from pit stacks, he found childhood recollections continued to tug his inventiveness and that year he sold one of his degree exhibits, 'Roger, Roger,' a sculpture of two men dressed in the uniforms of Cudworth Secondary School, to a collector in Basle in Switzerland.

Life at the college was not all work. The Central School of Art lads were invited to play darts with the Royal College in the students' common room, but Graham and a pal from the school of art became bored. Challenging his opponent to hit the dartboard with a beer mat, Graham was startled to see a table heading towards the target and the scene turned into a spat; tempers boiled and tables were overturned. The following day Graham was carpeted and the rector said that he would get a life ban from the students' bar if anything like that happened again. On another occasion a nearby householder was told where to get off on complaining to Graham and his pals about their boisterous singing in the street. This time the rector had had enough and imposed the ban. It was all very embarrassing for the next day Graham received a £750 cheque for winning the Madame Tussaud's Award for Figurative Art for outstanding work and the rector swallowed his pride and praised his work. He was in trouble again during the era of punk. The Sex Pistols, The Damned and Johnny and the Nose Bleeds all played at the college and during the performance by the Nose Bleeds Graham, like everyone else, threw a beer can at the band; but, unlike everyone else, Graham was singled out by the lead singer and punched on the nose. The irony of the band's title was not lost on him.

'College made me interact with other artists and people from other colleges and departments. There were at least two Turner Prize winners, Richard Deacon and Tony Cragg, who passed through college. We were also living in the right place, for every week my wife and children had the chance to go to nearby museums. We were in South Kensington and the Royal College's painting school had once been an annexe to the Victoria and Albert Museum. Getting into the Royal College changed my life. My two daughters had a similar impact. I have never thought of children as a burden and I have used them in my work: the young Graham Ibbeson, my children and comic children. My son Max was born in 1983 and was used to model the figure of William Webb Ellis. Now I have a grandchild and am inspired by her as well.'

Galleries as well as museums were an attraction while he was in London. A group of students invited to a private viewing at a well-known hoity-toity gallery in the Strand afterwards caught the No 14 bus back to Knightsbridge and South Kensington; well two of his mates boarded the double decker but the lad in the rear, Graham, had a problem. The bus was moving, he grabbed the pole on the platform, but his knees were at times scraping the road. The conductor laughed, shouting: 'Let go.' This timely advice was

A footstool, his first work at Trent Polytechnic. It was said to have been influenced by the word toadstool as in gnomes. *Ibbeson Collection*

The infamous and evil-looking gnomes who appear to have had a bad night on the booze. The first of his adopted 'families'. *Ibbeson Collection*

A scene close to his heart. The plaster characters are engaged in darts and playing the piano in a pub with sawdust on the floor. *Ibbeson Collection*

Carol and the children (Faye is on the left) visit Graham in his studio during his first year at the Royal College. There is a self portrait on the wall. Graham used his own hair to give the figure an authentic look. *Ibbeson Collection*

Faye and Emma in the park. *Ibbeson Family Archive*

'Wrestling Babies' – his first sale. *Ibbeson Collection*

The unfinished motorbike and naked woman statue which left Professor Meadows rubbing his chin in bewilderment. But it was a sign that Graham's restless imagination and burgeoning talent had moved on from gnomes and traditional statues. Again the imagery had been plucked from a whirlpool of influences in his childhood. *Ibbeson Collection*

ignored, fear took over and Graham's grip on the pole tightened as the vehicle rumbled past the gallery where a few minutes earlier he had musing on sophisticated aspects of art. It was like a scene out of a Laurel and Hardy film. The bus did stop and the conductor, being a fair man, said that Graham could pay a cheaper fare because he had boarded in a different fare zone to his pals. On arriving home Graham tried to explain to Carol why there were large ragged holes in the knees of his jeans.

People often confuse the Royal Academy of Art with the Royal College of Art, an error which on several occasions Graham has been reluctant to correct. An official of the London Symphony Orchestra, who wanted a large sculpture of the Viennese composer Johann Strauss for a New Year's Eve concert at the Albert Hall, was under the impression he was phoning the Academy but got Graham instead, the only figurative sculptor at the Royal College. He completed the 9ft-high work in two weeks. A similar mix-up in communications led to Graham producing a piece of art for the Commonwealth Institute.

The work ethic was beginning to take over. In 2010 Graham read a newspaper feature about Jack Vettriano, the artist who was born in a mining village in Scotland in the same year as Graham, 1951. Copies of his work sell in their millions. Graham said the words could have been written by him. Vettriano told the *Daily Mail*: 'I was obsessed by it (work ethic). The way I used to work could not be sustained. Sometimes I would be up at 3 o' clock in the morning, just put a cushion down on the studio floor and put a blanket over me, not bothering to take my clothes off, have a nap for an hour, then get up and start working again.'

There would be periods in the future when Graham found himself equally exhausted and mentally punch drunk: 'When I was doing The White Cliffs project the work was so intense that I felt like driving over the cliff into the sea.'

Before he left college Graham was offered a vision of life in Basildon in Essex. His degree exhibition was seen by a man in authority who was so excited by the originality of his work he offered him a part-time teaching job, a subsidised workshop and a council house in this planner's paradise where the town and life seemed to be mapped out in patterns. Graham was not sure what to do at first, though any doubts about staying were rinsed on reading a risible headline in the local newspaper: 'Beatniks move to Basildon.' It was a direct reference to the family. He looked at his fresh faced daughters in their pretty dresses and tidy and neat hairstyles and wondered: 'What's all this about?' There was something disconcertingly unfamiliar about the place, he concluded, so the family went back North.

There were other compelling reasons behind the decision to uproot but Barnsley was where everything was familiar and the town and mining villages were self sufficient, homely and welcoming to their own. But the beatnik comment still rankles in 2010.

A work of art on display at his degree course at the Royal College. He described it as a working-class grandfather clock. The cuckoo was based on the Rolls Royce trade mark and the chains inside the clock were marked 'toilet' and 'plumbing'. *Ibbeson Collection*

'No Such Park' … that was the title of this work. Graham based part of the scene on an old London Underground map he found in a skip. The children are looking for a park and are lost and end up tired at a bus stop. One of them is looking at the map and discovers there is 'no such park'. *Ibbeson Collection*

After all the word invokes the 1950s not the 1970s and perhaps tells you more about the ageing sub editor who wrote the headline rather than the appearance of the family. It was not grim up North anymore ('You can grin up North,' says Graham) and the family travelled up country on his 27th birthday in 1978, buttressed by the conviction the Royal College had changed his life and things would not be the same again: 'Before I was accepted at the college my back was against the wall.' A new home, a small house with a former plumber's workshop, and a part-time lecturer's job at Leeds Polytechnic awaited him. Some people have thought it was an extraordinary move. He was leaving London, where the arts flourished, and Barnsley was seen as both an industrial and artistic wasteland. Only an artist with talent and determination would survive there, said his friends. Graham was once again taking the arduous route in life but he also realised that this unusual town was a fruitful source of inspiration.

Powerful and funny imagery continued to be produced by Graham after college and he found himself intuitively in tune with large sectors of the public who identified with his slant on childhood and what he calls 'his gags'. Much of his humour has its origins in the old industrial towns with their factory chimneys, sooty mills, pits and flat capped comedians who thrived on the jokes and language of working class people. But his appeal has a wider base than those music hall funny men who rarely found an audience South of Watford Gap, and his overriding quality is that he seems to cross cultures. His Northern roots have struck a chord with a sizeable chunk of his clientèle who live abroad and his work has found its way into galleries and middle-class homes all over Europe and the USA. At the time it was seen as ground breaking stuff.

Three early statues embraced the universal and naive optimism of children – and adults – who try to find a way to the stars by flying out of the garden with the aid of improvised wings. He created 'The Wrong Brothers', as opposed to the Wright Brothers, a pair of adult characters with flat caps, cardboard wings and large November 5th rockets strapped to their backs; 'Quasiflymo', a caricature of Quasimodo with a propeller on his head (that figure was bought by an admirer living in Paris), and 'The Grimethorpe Flyer', a boy with cardboard wings.

'The Grimethorpe Flyer' has been a recurring theme throughout his forty-year career. The name derives from the nickname for the late night bus from Barnsley to Grimethorpe which, in fact, terminated at the bus depot in Shafton several miles short of Grimethorpe. That nickname is the only connection between the bus and his art work. The first version dates back to the days of his degree course and there have been variations since including a life-sized one in bronze now in a house near Illkley. Another is in the Tokyo Toy Museum where it's known as 'The Swine Cycle Kid'. Originally bought by the London Toy Museum, it depicts a boy with cardboard wings and goggles on a tricycle strapped to a small pig which is being encouraged to trot as fast as possible to give the lad the momentum to take off. At one point it was known as 'The Pork Cycle Kid', but the owner of the toy museum was Jewish and the work was re-named before ending up in Japan.

Back on the ground his feet were rooted in the grim industrial wasteland on his doorstep. He produced in 1980 'The Redundant Fairy' which symbolised the decline and then the collapse of the steel industry. The figure had rusting wings and a wand. It appeared in an exhibition, 'Woman', sponsored by the Playboy Club in Munich, Germany, though Graham is quick to point out his work did not have any of the features usually associated with the sensual ladies who sprawl across the pages of this magazine: 'You could just see her knees and bit of cleavage.' That sculpture was bought by a collector in New York.

Next stop was America where he realised a boyhood dream to view skyscrapers at close quarters and where his eyes and mind were also dazzled by the glittering world of art. Then it was back to hard graft in Barnsley.

Chapter 3

New York, New York

The first attempt to get Graham's work shown in America had a bizarre birth. He did not know about an exhibition which he was said to be staging there. While working as a part-time lecturer at Leeds Polytechnic he was told there was a large ad in a glossy magazine, *Art in America*, about this forthcoming and exciting event. Graham was bewildered. His name was in bold print but he had never been in touch with any gallery in America. What was going on? Was it an expensive prank? To add to the mystery, the ad featured a picture of his work, 'Roger, Roger', which had already been sold in Switzerland. It transpired a friend, Don Johnson, who lived on the outskirts of Chicago and who had been studying international law in London while Graham was at the Royal College, had been to a gallery in Chicago and told them about this remarkable artist from Barnsley.

But Graham, though grateful for his friend's assistance, did not like the terms under which the exhibition would be staged on the grounds he would have to pay for the transportation of his exhibits to America, and trying to control events taking place 3,000 miles away would have been difficult. Unknown to Graham at the time, he would soon be back there, this time travelling Pullman class, but first of all he did what many other members of his generation were doing and toured the US on the cheap.

In 1979 Graham and a pal known as Irish Bob decided to see what was happening over there. On arriving in New York his companion lost his passport and money and for the rest of the stay Graham had to subsidise him. During the fourteen-day sojourn by Greyhound bus they went to New Orleans and Washington, often having to sleep on the coach, and visited the gallery mentioned in the ad in Chicago. Money was tight, they wanted to see the sights and the return flight was days away, so in Washington they selected the longest ride they could go on a Greyhound ticket without having to pay for a hotel. The destination was Florida where they paddled in the sea for two hours before heading back to New York. On the return flight they were so hungry they had to keep asking the cabin crew for more food and at Manchester Airport he had just enough money to get to Piccadilly to phone Carol, who went to Barnsley rail station to pay for his ticket on the last leg of his trip. The exhibition did not go ahead.

A life-size statue entitled 'Workers' Playtime'. The character on the left was modelled on his father-in-law, Charlie, one of Graham's instant mates. *Freddy Neptune Limited*

'The Bone Ranger'. *Freddy Neptune Limited*

On his second visit to New York he was treated like royalty. Not that he had a lot of money in 1982: he had to borrow a corduroy jacket from his dad before leaving. Twelve artists were taken on an all-expenses trip from London to the Arnold Katzen Gallery in 11 East 5 Street in New York, where their exhibition entitled 'Superhumanism' was held. It turned out to be a breathless round of receptions, swanky restaurants and trips in limousines. As he toured the city he peered at the towering blocks of concrete and glass, some of which were as familiar as old haunts having helped to form his childhood world, while images of his work on posters advertising the arrival of the artists gazed down from large and countless billboards.

The vibrant noise of the city, the glamour, and the dizzying pace of life there were in sharp contrast to the days when as a thirteen-year-old he had pored over American comics in a drab mining village and thrilled at the pictures of Superman rescuing women from the tops of burning skyscrapers. This VIP visit to the city – as opposed to the earlier trip on the cheap – was the fulfilment of a resolutely sustained dream.

A wonderful study of two boys preparing to fight, an everyday scene in a mining village. It was entitled 'Bovver Boys'. A photograph of the statue was used to promote an exhibition in New York. The boys are attired in Cudworth Secondary Modern School uniforms. A poster featuring 'The Bovver Boys' went on sale on e-bay in 2010 but the Americans who owned it had a problem with the word 'Bovver' and the blurb referred to the 'Bower Boys'). *Freddy Neptune Limited*

The excitement of that short visit soon dissolved but the exhibition helped to sell 'The Bovver Boys' (two brothers 'knocking hell out of each other') and 'The Redundant Fairy'. This time in the US hunger was no longer a nagging companion and he had money in his pocket as he strapped himself into his seat for the return flight.

Between 1977 and 1992 Nicholas Treadwell exhibited his work all over America including New York, LA, Chicago and Miami and across Europe and in Hong Kong, though there were no all expenses trips or high octane receptions for the artists ('Artists have a tendency to drink too much,' says Graham). In 1980, however, having seen an offer whereby he could collect Persil washing coupons in exchange for rail tickets, he went to Paris on the cheap and stayed at a nondescript hostel. That's how he got the chance to exhibit his sculptures at the Grand Palais, alongside the work of Picasso. 'After that I boasted I had exhibited with Picasso, though I did not say I got there thanks to Persil.'

Meanwhile, two more pieces, 'Workers' Playtime' (a twenty-stone char lady dancing with a ten-stone plumber) and 'The Bone Ranger' (a masked bulldog riding a rocking horse), both on show at an art fair in New York, were bought by the owner of the Studio 53 gallery on Park Avenue, Linda Gottlieb, and went on display in her apartment. Years later in 1992 Graham's daughter, Emma, was unhappy working as a nanny over there so Graham, Carol and Max flew over in the New Year (1993) with the intention of bringing her back. At one point, killing time before the flight, he went into Studio 53 dressed in a leather jacket and baseball cap and the staff wondered who he was. The walls dripped with the prints of Picasso and the luxuriant works of other twentieth-century artists. As he spoke to staff and tried to find the courage to tell them that his work had been on display there years before, the owner overheard Graham and realised who he was. That meeting resulted in nine of his works being shipped from the UK to America where they went on show at the gallery. All were later bought by the owner. 'I did not get my cheque at that time so I had to go over again and collect it, but that turned out to be another excuse to see America and have a drinking spree with the lads who went along as well.'

His biggest job in the 1980s originated not in an artistic crucible like New York or Paris but on his doorstep in York, where he produced forty life-sized figures for the Jorvik Viking Centre. It was the first themed museum in the country, reflecting the period of invasion from Scandinavia, and was the brainchild of John Sunderland, a genius according to Graham. His connection with the project started when applying for a job at Barnsley Art School where two members of the board were his former lecturers from 1967. The old question came up: 'Why do you want to be a teacher?' He gave the same answer as in the past: 'To subsidise my work as an artist.' Again it was the wrong answer. The post went to Steve West, who had been to the Royal Academy of Art and on a scholarship to Rome. Both Graham and Steve had a joint exhibition at the Cooper Art Gallery, Barnsley, 'Slapstick and Witty', which was featured on BBC's *Look North*. The people who were doing the Jorvik project saw the programme and Steve was asked to create the figures, a job he declined because he did not want to leave the art school. Steve said Graham might like to do the work and that was the beginning of what could be termed a gloriously productive era.

The contract was lucrative. Before a start could be made Graham and Carol had to move all their furniture out of the living room of their detached home in Doncaster Road, Barnsley, black out the windows and install spotlights to put on a temporary exhibition for the benefit of the men behind the Jorvik. When asked to view his workshop, he took them outside to the carport and a polythene sheet. About twelve months were spent on producing the models in a former industrial unit at Wakefield which was rented by the organisers for that purpose. His old friends, the stern looking gnomes from college days, had given him valuable experience. His task was to create thirty Vikings, not the pillaging or raping variety, but an ancient version of boring Joe Public engaged in play and on chores in a village, everything from children running and playing to women doing house work. He trawled his local pub for suitable victims on which to base his fibre glass figures; so the Viking peering at the tourists from the tableau in the museum could well have had its origins in a character having a pint in a bar in Barnsley. To add the zany Ibbeson touch he sat a caricature of American comedian WC Fields on a primitive toilet. The museum was a resounding success and the visitors flocked there, just as they did years later when the Eric Morecambe statue boosted trade in the resort of Morecambe.

Back in 1983 Graham did other figures, this time props for a Kenny Everett film, *Bloodbath at the House of Death*, which included a fibreglass chef with a cleaver buried in his skull. Graham drove from Wakefield to York with the lifelike figure sat next to him in his open topped 2 CV Citroen, an uneventful journey which failed to raise any semblance of alarm among motorists. The film, also starring Vincent Price, was a ninety-two-minute spoof on horror films: eighteen people were killed off in eighteen different ways. Unlike the museum in York, the film was a flop.

Thanks to his Vikings, Graham and Carol found themselves 'in front as far as money was concerned' for just about the first time in their married life. Their finances may have been put on a much sounder footing but the hard work was beginning to take its toll. Embarking on a new figure based on the comedian of the 1920s and 1930s, WC Fields, he found his mental and creative elasticity stretched to the limit. In an intemperate mood he smashed the figure, hurled the parts into a skip along with his work clothes,

This is based on one of Graham's favourite American comedians, W C Fields, who was famous in the 1930s but whose popularity waned in the 1950s; he was 'discovered' again in the 1960s by students and film critics who became avid fans of his old films. He was a former juggler who annoyed studio producers in the 1930s by trying to include a juggling act in a film based on a Charles Dickens' book. This work is entitled 'Balls'. *Freddy Neptune Limited*

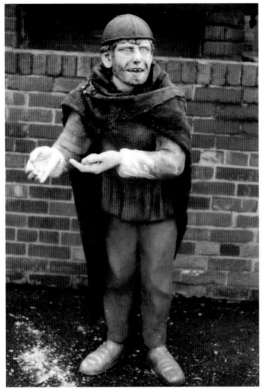

Viking work in progress in Graham's backyard.
Ibbeson Collection

First day at work at York. John Sunderland, the brains behind this groundbreaking idea of a Viking museum, is second right. *Ibbeson Collection*

and in his underwear walked indoors to take a shower, almost as though he was trying to discard his old life. He said candidly: 'I have finished.'

The outburst was supposed to herald a permanent break from his craft. In reality it may have been a warning he was on the brink of nervous exhaustion and needed a rest: even today he says that having a studio at home is like living above the shop and relaxation at home can be difficult at times ('The trouble is that the work is solitary and no one calls at the shop'). Having destroyed Mr Fields, he remained becalmed and cloistered for three weeks before continuing to develop what he calls his gift and curse with a new sense of enthusiasm. As he says: 'You cannot give up art.'

The mid 1980s proved to be productive, not just for the Viking museum contract, but for the aftermath of the miners' strike. The 1984/85 upheaval in the coal industry turned out to be a double edged sword. Given his background, he found the dispute unsettling.

Carol was again the principal model when Graham produced this mining tableau at Conisbrough, near Doncaster. She is the grieving widow and a figure of a miner is seen emerging out of the ground. *Ibbeson Collection/Brian Elliott*

Standing the test of time: the figures outside the National Union of Mineworkers' offices in Huddersfield Road, Barnsley. The statues have become a familiar part of the townscape, so familiar that motorists and pedestrians do not give them a second look. Yet they are still meaningful and evocative. *Ibbeson Collection/Brian Elliott*

After the strike the defeated mining communities seemed to release a spurt of collective emotion and a yearning for the past. This communal catharsis enabled him to embark on projects which helped to preserve at least the spirit of the old way of life.

A miners' strike was nothing new in the family. During one of the two big confrontations between the union and the coal board in the early 1970s his father triggered one of the early flare-ups between miners and police. He went to the pit to collect his wages and walked onto a picket line. A lorry driver who was trying to break the blockade ran over and broke his mate's leg and in retaliation his dad hurled a brick through the windscreen, much to the disgust or delight of the police who marched him off to Cudworth police station. Tempers were boiling and the police, fearing the furious pickets would storm the police station, transferred him to the cells at Wombwell, a few miles away. Arthur Scargill, then an official of the Yorkshire miners' union, paid the court fine.

Graham working on a miner which formed part of the Hucknall work of art. It is the highest free-standing sculpture in Nottinghamshire. *Ibbeson Collection*

The incident on the picket line was filmed by a television camera crew and his dad appeared in a murky clip on *News at Ten*, watched by millions of viewers, many of whom were startled to see on television for the first time violent images of industrial unrest in the UK. In the coalfields it was seen as a minor detonation in a corner of a village. Graham's mum had a more down-to-earth perspective: at a distance she had seen the commotion on the picket line and had casually told friends and neighbours that some silly so-and-so had been causing trouble at the pit, not realising her husband was the culprit who had been carted off to the cells. Graham was more philosophical. When asked: 'Have you appeared on television?' his proud boast at that time was: 'No; but my dad has been on *News at Ten*.'

By the time the big strike started in March 1984, Graham had been out of the industry for nearly twenty years. However, members of his family still worked in the pits; his father did not accept redundancy until after the strike at the age of fifty-four. His aunt helped with distribution of food parcels and Graham provided part-time work for his brother-in-law who was a mineworker. Few people who have been brought up in a mining village can remain coolly detached from what went on during that dispute and he was no exception. The relationship between the NCB and miners had been like a powder keg for years, tremulously waiting for detonation. The sudden decision to close Cortonwood Colliery, near Barnsley, provided the fuse and spark. There was violence on both sides of the picket lines, about 11,000 miners were arrested and 7,000 injured.

The divisions in the communities ran silent and deep. Men who went back to work before the union decided to do so were ostracised and even attacked by bitter enders. In 2008, there were two brothers who lived near each other in Barnsley who had not spoken to each since the 1984 strike: one was a union man, the other had tried to go to work shortly after the dispute started. There was even the case of a man who had been barred from his club in the 1926 miners' lock-out for strike breaking; he was still barred fifty years later. Since the miners' defeat almost all the pits have gone. The 150-year-old Barnsley coalfield, which had employed 16,000 in the early 1980s, closed in the early 1990s: the last to go was the colliery where Graham's grandfather had worked, Grimethorpe.

The last remnants of a way of life disappeared with the pits. Graham tried to make sense of it all in his work. He suggested a monument, 'The Coal Queen', a towering figure of a woman in bronze panelling, on the back of which would be a miniature model of pit head gear and cascading imitation coal. Her hand would have clasped a pick. The suggested site was the former spoil heap at Dodworth, near Barnsley, which could be seen by motorists on the M1. Had the proposal been approved, Graham says it would have been a statue of an attractive woman, 'my version of Mother Earth or Mother Coal'. It would have been years ahead of its time, a Barnsley version of 'The Angel of the North'.

In 1986 Carol, who was becoming an experienced model, was in action again, this time being used for another mining figure, at Conisbrough, in memory of a former miner, lecturer and leader of Doncaster Borough Council, Jim MacFarlane, who had died suddenly in 1985, aged fifty-five. Commissioned by the MacFarlane Trust and Doncaster Library Service, it featured in bronze a barefoot and grief-stricken woman in a shawl, situated a few feet from a dying miner who is emerging from the ground, the victim of a roof fall. 'The woman is facing the reality of what's left behind after the death of the man. I tried to get across the determination of the woman to go on with life. It must have worked. At the unveiling my mother and father cried when they saw the figure.'

The memorial proved to be controversial and there were protest placards at the unveiling ceremony. 'The image was too near the bone and too stark. People were being reminded every day about what had happened in the past, but that anger did not last. Within twelve months the people who had protested at the unveiling were helping to look after the memorial. I have known all about death and the frailty of life and I knew I could do the memorial with compassion. But my work is not all about grief, I use humour in other work to get away from this stark reality.'

By 1992 the National Union of Mineworkers had commissioned three life-size figures in bronze on granite: a grieving mother with babe in arms, representing the past; a modern miner and a child from the 1950s. Sited outside the union offices in Barnsley, the figures exemplified the fortitude of miners' families and reminded the public of the grief that had soured communities in the past. There were other memorials, at Hucknall in Nottinghamshire and at South Kirkby near Pontefract. The Nottinghamshire bronze miner is 12ft-high, a warrior-type figure perched on top of a miner's lamp. Again the memorial involved Graham's family: the 'warrior' was modelled on his son Max and the life-size figure of a Victorian miner inside the miner's lamp on Graham's father. At the unveiling the widow of a miner killed down the pit, on seeing the statues, wept. The memorial, commissioned by the Nottingham County Council, Ashfield District Council and Tesco, is the highest free standing statue in Nottinghamshire. In 2010, Graham is still working on a mining memorial, this time at Kellingley Colliery, near Pontefract, though he believes the public mood for such tributes is cooling as memories of the pits die. However the industry refuses to release its grip on him: 'I have this recurring dream of a miner falling or emerging from a wall of coal, perhaps a body that is part of the coal and can't escape.'

The Hucknall sculpture waiting to be cast in bronze at the foundry. Also pictured are the workers in the foundry, skilled men and women who have won Graham's admiration. *Ibbeson Collection*

The magnificent Hucknall statue is now a much appreciated landmark in the former Nottinghamshire mining town. Detail of the old miner can be seen in the close-up image. *Brian Elliott*

Chapter 4

Eric Presley and Fame

Slapstick humour is Graham's lifeblood. He has admired a medley of comedians and cartoon characters including Laurel and Hardy, Eric Morecambe, The Bash Street Kids, the saucy Bamforth and Don McGill seaside postcard figures and Tom and Jerry. Those influences have helped to produce a series of work which included in 1985 his tribute to the traditional char lady, 'Sculpt Char', a fibre glass monument which had two char ladies cleaning a larger version of this formidable breed. That same year came 'The Lost Monument' depicting four hilariously incompetent Boy Scouts who are lost. One figure stands on top of the plinth, clasping in one hand a compass on which there is no face while the others stand underneath peering into the distance, nonplussed by East and West which seem to have gone haywire. The statue, positioned in the bushes at the Yorkshire Sculpture Park, was an unsuspecting and refreshing sight for visitors who had lost their sense of direction as well.

He has the gift to turn the innocuous, incongruous and implausible into works of art. While having a drink in the former Wheatsheaf pub in Barnsley he watched the landlady's son, Nathan, aged about five, come down the stairs leaving behind a meandering trail of red handprints. He and his cousin's inept attempt to decorate a room with emulsion left his parents fuming and the clientele laughing. Graham turned the incident into a study of an angry mother carrying a son who has tried to please her by doing her portrait on paper but who has been too liberal with the paint – there is a sizeable splash on her backside. In another statue, a visually intriguing and moving work, a forlorn runaway boy is painting as he sits at a bus stop with his only possessions. That idea is based on an incident in childhood when Graham and his sister ran away from home. He put 'Ar Ugly' (she called him a Tommy Tormentor), then aged two, in his trusty trolley and pushed her through the village. He ran out of puff on a nearby steep hill and the great escape was abandoned.

The mischievous power struggle between children was crystallised in the George and Eric series. His cousin, Paul Thwaites, who was almost like a brother, was sometimes a target. Their antics have found their way into his work. In 'Pain in the Neck' Graham depicts a scene in which the older boy has asked his brother to look at the sky while using a catapult to smack his victim on the head. Graham says this work is about brotherly love, deviousness and gullibility. Even dreams have played a part in his work. In one dream, while walking around the foundry where his sculptures are made, he spotted a model of golden eagle on a work bench: 'From the back the baby is holding onto the wings. From one side the image looks like an eagle, like a baby from the other side and from yet another angle the baby appears to be flying.' A few weeks later Graham had visitors, Bruce Collins and his wife, who asked what he was working on. 'I told him about the dream and that I had not started on the work yet; he wrote out a cheque and announced: "Your dream has come true".' The finished work, 'Babe of Prey,' went to the visitors' home in Middlesex. The couple later moved to New Zealand and the 10ft-high eagle is now at a nursing home over there.

'My work either concentrates on the comic or tragic and there is nothing in between. In the same way the beautiful is contrasted with the ugly.' Graham believes most humans can empathise with ugly people and that's why he went through a phase of constructing kids with bulldog faces, their facial expressions resembling 'an ugly woman chewing a wasp'. Sometimes he just concentrates on bulldogs. One of the first of that genre was sold immediately in Madrid: a bulldog is portrayed playing tennis with a frying pan, to the bottom of which is stuck the egg and bacon, another example where surrealism, anarchic humour and Graham's inventiveness have conspired to produce art. Dogs have played a part in his work and at home, too. The Ibbesons had their own ugly dog for a time, a kind of refugee from a Tom and Jerry cartoon and a favourite with the growing family. Beano was a deaf albino boxer, an unlikely guard dog. Though he could not hear the traffic passing the house he picked up the vibrations and spent his time trying to kill buses. One day, when prowlers had been reported behind the house, the police called and Graham awakened Beano on the sofa before the officers could sit down. 'You have got a good guard dog there,' grinned one of the officers.

By the early 1990s his work was on view at the Yorkshire Sculpture Park. One statue marked the 150th anniversary of the invention of photography, with his favourite model, Carol, as usual, a picture of serenity. The comical side to the feature was provided by a laughing boy, who is holding a Kodak Brownie 127 camera, and a sobbing girl. The boy had incited the girl to tears to get a classic and spontaneous photograph, an example of Graham's theme of 'brotherly and sisterly love, deviousness and gullibility'. Hidden in nearby bushes were statues of the dependable old firm, George and Eric. 'I remember people tittering in the bushes. They were not amorous couples but people who had come across George and Eric.'

The exhibition at the Marcus Marcus gallery in Amsterdam proved to be the most popular commercial exhibition in that city in 1991. His humour caught the imagination

'Sculpt Char' … two char ladies are helping to clean a monument dedicated to the old fashioned char lady. Graham has added the Ibbeson touch by putting a crow on the broom and bird droppings on the plinth. *Yorkshire Sculpture Park*

'Lost monument' … this piece was ordered by a shopping complex in LA, America, but was never collected. It later went on show at the Yorkshire Sculpture Park. *Yorkshire Sculpture Park*

'Self Portrait' … Graham at a bus stop. It's loosely based on an incident when he tried to run away from home. In this work the figure has grabbed all his favourite possessions – including a cricket bat - rather than essentials such as clothes and food, a sign perhaps the act of rebellion was merely a gesture and that soon he would return home. *Nicholas Treadwell Gallery*

'Pain in the Neck' … George and Eric, two comic strip-type characters based on Graham and his cousin Paul. They were mischievous pals. *Freddy Neptune Limited*

'Eye of the Beholder' … the statue marking the 150th anniversary of the invention of the camera. This early work demonstrates his growing preoccupation with classical figures as well as characters influenced by seaside postcards and comics. *Yorkshire Sculpture Park*

Entitled 'A portrait of the Artist with Artist's Mum with Portrait of Artist's Mum'. *Ibbeson Collection*

'Wife on an Ocean Wave' … Lost at sea but later retrieved and given pride of place in Cardiff. *Freddy Neptune Limited*

of the public, perhaps because saucy seaside postcards were popular in Europe before they became a craze in the UK in the twentieth century. The gallery was near a canal and his work had a theme associated with the sea, water and bath nights from yesteryear. The pieces included 'Wife on the Ocean Wave', a bronze replica of which almost had a watery grave; 'George and Eric'; and 'North Sea Jerry', based on an old tin bath converted into a vessel.

Tin baths fascinate Graham. By the time he was growing up they were obsolescent as working-class families moved into new council houses with the then ultimate luxuries, bathrooms and electricity. Children in the 1950s found that discarded baths could be turned into sloops fit for fledgling pirates en route to the Spanish Main or converted into liners – it depended on the volatility and breadth of their imaginations. Large baths became two or three seaters and a sweeping brush was erected to make a mast. 'We found baths left in gardens and took them to the local quarry and pretended we were crossing the Atlantic to New York. Those symbols of poverty became play things when they were thrown away. I have a romantic vision when it comes to tin baths, for when I see a vessel I think of a tin bath.'

The exhibition cost £2,000 per week to keep open. It was a lavish affair, tin baths apart, and the private viewing was attended by leading figures in the fashion world and in TV, an appreciative audience whose cosmopolitan tastes chimed with his earthy caricatures from the North of England. While champagne glasses were raised and emptied among the glamorous and renowned, Graham remained loyal to the English pub and draught. The organisers knew he preferred beer to wine and export strength Guinness was brought in. 'One of my mates claimed it was 13 per cent proof and when he had a sup he went bright red in the face, you could see the blood rising.' His father-in-law Charlie, however, was on a more elevated plain: he was on the point of becoming a minor celebrity in Holland. One of the statues, with Charlie as one of the two figures, was used in the opening sequence to a Dutch television series. Charlie, the former miner with his hair parted down the middle, was in coat and tails with L-plates on his back and was dancing with an Angel. Even Graham wonders about the type of subterranean creative impulse that gives birth to such a fascinating combination of dancers.

A cavalcade of funny exhibits followed the exhibition in Holland. 'Last Rumba in Rotherham' unleashed onto the public a Carmen Miranda-type figure, with a bunch of fruit and vegetables poised on her head, dancing with Charlie the sailor. Graham's love of the sea and makeshift sails continued with an outrageous and unromantic version of The Spanish Main in 'Shipshape': a bulldog with a wooden leg and a parrot on his shoulder are on a raft which has a sweeping brush as a mast and a telescope made of old tin cans. The treasure map has locations like Dog-caster, Rover-ham and Nashers-ville .

Meanwhile, 'Eric Presley', a denim-jacketed character standing on a plinth that looked like a juke box, made things rock and buzz for the wrong reasons on his appearance at the Glynn Vivian Art Gallery in Swansea. Unfortunately bees found their way under the blue suede shoes and made a hive, much to the consternation of the staff who called in a beekeeper. For once Graham was outgunned in puns by the specialists in madcap headlines, the subeditors on *The Sun* newspaper, who used 'Eric Presley All Shook Up' at the top of the story. The exhibit, minus live bees, was taken to the Nicholas Treadwell gallery, then in Bradford. 'Eric', now becoming as embarrassing as the stereotype younger brother who whiffs, overturned the artistic apple cart there by creating a pong rather than a buzz. Visitors to the vegetarian cafe complained of a funny smell and the finger was pointed at poor old 'Eric', who had become a repository for dead insects and maggots. Like the black sheep of a family at a party he was sent home in disgrace.

'Just About Married' did not cause any embarrassment – it brought a smile to guests at a four star hotel in Linz, Austria. Having a passing reference to a saucy seaside postcard, the statue portrayed a buxom woman kissing her new and highly nervous husband on the head: it was the first item spotted by newly arrived guests including honeymooners at the hotel and had been bought by the owners to amuse the clientèle.

The bronze version of 'Wife on an Ocean Wave', commissioned by the Cardiff Bay Development Corporation (1993), nearly went down without trace. Ensconced in a frail tin bath on the sea, an overweight woman is holding hands with a smaller man at the top end and there is a baby in a sailor suit trying to catch a fish. On arrival in Cardiff the statue was put on a site on the dockside, after which someone tried to steal it for scrap and the council decided to find another location. It was placed in a supposedly safe compound for a temporary period but then disappeared. Six months later at low tide the statue was spotted in the bay. 'It was hoisted out and I was asked to view it before being re-sited. It was covered in barnacles and the bronze had gone green. I was told it needed renovating but I said: 'No; it looks fantastic' and it was sited, barnacles and all, on the dockside at Cardiff Bay.'

Most of his humorous work has been in fibreglass, but there is nothing funny about the after effects of using this material, a curse which has stalked his health for years. As a student he used plaster and the models were then broken up. For years he could not afford to work in bronze and fibre glass enabled him to use bright colours which added to the humour. 'It is wonderful because you are the master of your own destiny. I sculpted in clay, cast into fibreglass, painted the work and then offered it to the world in an exhibition. The downside to this is that after working in the material for forty years, and extensively in the 1980s and 1990s, I am ill when I use resin and fibre glass. My chest becomes heavy and I get headaches even when using a mask.'

He was caught in the aftermath of a chemical fire when exhibiting at Stratford-upon-Avon. The exhibits, taken there in a van, were put display and he was in the hotel when there was the sound of a fire engine siren. 'At first I thought it was on *Eastenders* on the television in the hotel, but then there was banging on the door and someone shouted "The van is on fire". It was the hottest day of the year and the interior of the van had caught fire, it was probably the chemicals. The fire brigade managed to save the hired van and we

'Super Dog' ... He likes bulldogs because they remind him of ugly children. Everyone, he says, can empathise with ugly people or ugly animals. *Freddy Neptune Limited*

'Tennis Menace' ... A Tom and Jerry-type bulldog playing tennis (1979). *Freddy Neptune Limited*

came back to Barnsley all right and lost the deposit. That fire seemed to strip my sinuses; I no longer have a kind of natural filter system and that's why I become ill. On another occasion I was moving furniture from our then holiday home in Bridlington. It was 2000, my forty-ninth birthday. I came home very ill and after using the sink found it was full of blood. My sinuses were bleeding and it was all due to having worked in fibre glass.'

Luckily he can now afford to work in bronze which does not have health hazards – apart from the fact that it's heavy to move. He waxes lyrical about the process of casting in bronze. 'My first cast was while I was at the Royal College. I am a figurative sculptor and casting in bronze was the ultimate achievement. There is something magical about it. Tissa Ranasinge at the foundry near the college had taught me the rudimentary techniques. The first piece was a six-inches high portrait of my daughter, Faye, cross-

Mablethorpe: the Lincolnshire resort where Graham and Carol met. 'Flying down to Mablethorpe' was perhaps based on the title of the old Fred Astaire movie, *Flying Down to Rio. Ibbeson Collection*

'Last Rumba in Rotherham' … This was Doris Miranda as opposed to Carmen Miranda, a popular American singer in the 1940s and 1950s. Instead of having exotic fruit on her head, this singer sports cabbages and leeks. It's a curious mixture of Hollywood and Yorkshire influences. *Ibbeson Collection*

Charlie, with 'L' plates on the back, is dancing with an Angel. *Ibbeson Collection*

The clay version of the children setting off on the Jarrow March. *Ibbeson Collection*

legged on the floor with a party hat. I made another and sold them when I was on my uppers before I came back to Yorkshire.'

He had to wait from 1978 until the 1990s before working on his own bronze work again. His approach to sculpting had to change and he had to make 'the surface loose, more textured so that it reflected light.' The bronze foundry is a kind of an extension to his studio. The staff work in conjunction with the sculptor though the artist has to relinquish some control of his work. 'The process is expensive, labour intensive and the men are craftsmen, sculptors in their own right. I come from a working-class background and working in a foundry is physical work. Anyone from such a background believes in a way that a job is not real unless it's physical. I love foundry work. It has a different atmosphere. There is a smell of wax, plaster, rubber and dust; there is also the warmth of camaraderie. You have men, women, artists and craftsmen all working together. I feel as if I am part of an historic community when working in bronze. The basic wax technique has not changed since the days of the Etruscans, Greeks and Romans. Technology may have moved on but not the technique.'

His projects usually take about nine months from the day the instructions are given by clients to the installation of the statue. First of all the figure is modelled in clay. 'Most bronze sculptures and virtually all bronze statues are modelled in clay and on viewing a bronze I can tell the quality of the material of its birth. You can pinpoint the era when the piece was sculpted by the style of modelling. The Sir Francis Drake portrait on Plymouth Hoe is a perfect example. The figure with its immaculate modelling and clothing expertly sculpted in clay enables it to look ultra real in bronze and was produced in the Victorian age. That age produced that kind of discipline. The looser modelling of Jacob Epstein can be placed in the early twentieth century.

'Clay is the starting point in most of my projects and though I model occasionally in direct plaster clay is my preferred material for portraits. I have used 1120 buff body clay throughout my career. It is mid-grey with a little grit and suits my needs perfectly. There is nothing like the feel of a new bag of the stuff, the weight, the consistency; it's a cold elemental material. Then you feel the anticipation of a creative challenge. I have never found the challenge of sculpting clay daunting and all my doubts have been resolved when I open the first bag.

'A sculptor/carver can visualise his figure or image within the stone or wood before he starts work. The sculpture is there to be released from the 'mother' material by an expert. A sculptor/modeller builds up the sculpture by adding. I am an adder and not a taker away. When I get half a tonne of clay from the stockist I see the sculpture waiting in the bags. My challenge is to make this base material into a work of art. Clay has to be cast or fired. While sculpting you can keep it malleable by using a damp cloth and you can retain the moisture by covering it in plastic sheeting. If it gets too wet, it goes to slurry, too dry it cracks, falls apart and turns to dust and the sculpture is lost.'

One of the first tasks is to make a metal frame on which the clay is sculpted and the next job is to get the general shape of the figure. 'This takes a couple of days at the most and then I have to knuckle down and start refining the work. This can take as little as a few days but usually a month or so. With Laurel and Hardy I had it wrapped up for six months having spent a couple of months modelling the "boys", then I waited for the fans to inspect the work and for the funding to be raised. With Eric Morecambe I waited six years for the go ahead and it took less than a month to model while nursing Carol back to health. Clay is recyclable. After moulding I strip the clay off the frame, putting it in three large plastic tubs, damp it down and use it again. I do like to use new clay as the recycled stuff has remnants of former projects retained in its body (plaster and debris from the mould making process). All sculptors I have met and who use clay have expressed a longing to retain the visual elements of the original clay. The modelling is always sharper. Clay has a subtle, reflective quality as a result of water retention, making the shadows deeper and the surface more alive. The piece retains the finger and spatula marks made by the sculptor in his battle with the clay. But much of those qualities and subtleties are lost during the process of casting.'

Graham working on a clay figure for the 'children seen and not heard' theme at Northallerton hospital.
Ibbeson Collection

Benny Hill in clay. Graham used old and unwanted fire service buttons on which to base the 'F.S.' buttons for the uniform on the 'Fred Scuttle' statue (Fred was one of Benny's screen characters). *Ibbeson Collection*

The next step is to create a rubber mould of the clay figure and the mould is filled with wax. 'There is also a certain amount of anxiety when making a mould. If you make a balls up, the clay original is lost and the hard work disintegrates. I do not like mould making, it is a means to an end. I have made hundreds of moulds in plaster and rubber.'

In the foundry a ceramic shell is made around the wax figure after which the wax is melted and removed. A crucible is filled with liquid bronze which is poured into the ceramic shell investment (mould). Once it's cooled the figure needs several more minor modifications before the final cleaning and shaping takes place. The foundry is Graham's second home. He walks in as if it's an old haunt in Yorkshire and there is nothing quite as sweet as the first sighting of his bronze portrait of a public figure with its finely hewn features, an elegant and permanent work of art. That's when he knows all the work has been worthwhile.

'George and Eric the Half Brother' … George, the older brother, with the magician's top hat, demonstrates that Eric is really his half brother. *Freddy Neptune Limited*

Chapter 5

Sunshine in Morecambe

The public know Graham's work through the bronze sculptures now occupying prime sites in thirty cities and towns in the UK. But they do not realise many statues are erected without any ceremony at all; the excitement and celebrations at the Eric Morecambe unveiling were not the norm. His first public art work, a 10ft-high piece in Northampton (1986) was commissioned to provide a focal point in the new pedestrian precinct and to mark the town's links with the shoe industry.

His work centred on a large version of what's known as a hobbin-foot, a reminder of the days when most working-class homes used this implement to repair shoes and clogs, and on two running children based on Graham and his sister as children. The image was approved by the council and erected on a Sunday morning without any fanfare.

'I sat in the car, had a sandwich and then drove up the M1 back home. Afterwards I was told it had been downplayed because there had been opposition to the creation of the pedestrian precinct. It was my first major work in bronze and I was proud of it. It's an accolade to make a monument for a city but there is a downside. You have to live with the project for at least a year and the work causes a lot of stress; however, it is all worth it in the end.'

The following year he did Thomas Chippendale (1718-1779), the distinguished cabinet-maker whose bronze figure is shown admiring a section of one of his elegant chairs. It now stands in his home town of Otley in West Yorkshire.

'Scales of Justice', a magisterial combination of beauty (the maiden) and the beasts (the children) came in 1990. The statue, now standing outside the law courts in Middlesbrough, caused a public row because in 1987 there had been a scandal in Cleveland in which some parents had been wrongly accused of child sex abuse. Memories of social workers dragging children from their homes were fresh in the memory and a solicitor said the statue served as a reminder that Cleveland was still seen as the child abuse capital of the world. The council, however, defended it.

The figure of a woman holding two children by the scruff of their necks was misinterpreted by those who thought it was making a kind of statement about the infamous case. 'It was important; I tried to do something classical. It had

Graham and sister Gail seen as children at play. It's part of the statue at Northampton. Graham modelled in direct plaster instead of clay to give the statues a loose appearance. *Ibbeson Collection*

nothing to do with that case. It was about motherhood and the impartiality of motherhood; after all the violence was coming from the children. The woman had a serene look; she was a classical figure, pre-Raphaelite almost. The boy and girl looked like cartoon characters. Again there was no ceremony and the unveiling took place with just a couple of councillors present.' Graham compares the work of a public sculptor to that of being a plumber or builder: 'You do the job, make sure the statue is in the right place and then you are off without any fuss.'

His approach to public commissions differs depending on the project. 'I work hard on them all. Some were done purely for financial reward. I do not think I would have sculpted the Thomas Chippendale work if it had not been for the money which has subsidised my gallery work. I have embarked on others because they have been design challenges. I have to come up with my own interpretation of what is going to go into that open public space. You have to be creative and do something unique. It's also a battle. The Northampton project was advertised nationally and there was a long list never mind a short list before I won. I also enjoy the opportunity of working on the statues of my heroes like Eric Morecambe and Laurel and Hardy. There are other problems with

Thomas Chippendale. *Ibbeson Collection*

which to contend. Sometimes you have to use a structural engineer. For instance, if you are doing a statue of a cricketer bowling and balancing on one foot you have to make sure 500 kilograms of bronze are not going to topple over.'

There is one aspect of his work that bothers him. Like other artists he finds fault after a few years. He lives in a town where there are two of his sculptures on public view (the miners' family and Dickie Bird), both of which are near his home and sometimes he closes his eyes when passing. The faults, if indeed they are faults, would not be spotted by the public, there is nothing wrong with the pose, style, design or construction, just little things here and there that he can detect and which matter to a man who has an incorruptible urge to maintain mastery of his craft. 'As an artist you never stop learning or developing and what you did twenty years ago you would not do now. But as I have said before all artists keep looking at their work and finding fault.'

The project known as 'The White Cliffs Experience' was a major undertaking. He had sixteen weeks in which to sculpt forty pieces and at one point he was using Carol's hair drier to dry the varnish on some of the models before they were taken by van to Dover where the museum was established. The job also gave him the quirky satisfaction of portraying Captain Webb, the first man to swim the Channel (1875), whose image was on the box of matches he saw next to his father's Woodbine cigarettes when he was a child.

The museum covered the history of the port. It gave Graham the chance to work again with John Sunderland, who was behind the Jorvik Viking Centre at York, and who had approached him to do the work on the Kent coast in 1990. 'The idea was that of a hot air balloon carrying figures over the English Channel. In a couple of months this developed into a 'Carousel of Crossings', depicting the heroic and foolhardy attempts to cross from Dover to Calais and vice versa. I enlisted the skills of Martin Higson, who worked as a metalwork technician at Trent Poly – I knew him as a student there in the 1970s.

'John, Martin and I decided to represent the balloon by using steel rings of different dimensions with the small sculptures depicting the crossings attached to the rings. John gave me complete freedom to do the figures in my own style, the only stipulation being that they had to be based on actual crossings or attempted crossings. It was a perfect commission – I could be as daft as I wanted to be and get paid.'

Many of his familiar characters were rolled out for the occasion. Quasiflymo was trying to cross while he was strapped to a kite and W C Fields was doing the same in a whisky bottle. All were based on actual events – Graham just included his own characters. Alice in Wonderland, in a basket with other figures, was portrayed handing a sandwich to Captain Webb and alongside her were George and Eric eating fish and chips. The sculpture was enormous and extended down the stairwell with seaweed and 'fish' swimming in the metal sea. The White Cliffs Experience proved popular with visitors but closed in 1999.

Graham was soon involved with John Sunderland again, this time at the 'Eurotunnel Exhibition Centre'. The Channel Tunnel was behind schedule so an exhibition centre was suggested to show the public how it would look and work. He produced four large fibreglass wall reliefs and several life-sized figures. When the tunnel opened in 1994 there was no further use for the centre so closure followed.

Graham has discovered that on several occasions heartbreak can precede or follow a major work. After the opening of the centre in 1992 he arrived home to find his father had suffered a heart attack and was in intensive care. A few days later his mother, who was fretting about his father, had an angina attack and found herself in an adjoining ward.

His parents, like many of their generation who had lived in terraced or council houses, had an unfulfilled dream. They both wanted a bungalow 'where they could relax and potter around the garden'. His mother was discharged from hospital first and she pursued her Shangri La with a remarkable burst of energy, almost as though time was not on her side. She bought a bungalow in the next village with Dad's redundancy money and their savings without Granville having seen their new home. A solicitor visited the hospital so he could sign the papers. Having to keep his parents' stress levels to a minimum, Graham and his sister moved house for them.

'My parents moved in on the Monday but by the end of the week the dream had died. My mother passed away in her sleep on the Thursday night. She had spent fewer than four nights in the home of her dreams. My father lived another nine years.'

Like most people, Graham had spent part of his childhood impersonating Robin Hood or Little John, perhaps using a nearby wood as a makeshift Sherwood Forest. Most children modelled themselves on the dashing Errol Flynn version of the outlaw with the heart of gold, drawn from the Hollywood film made in the late 1930s. In the early 1990s Graham did his own version when asked by Nottinghamshire County Council to make life-sized figures of Robin and Little John fighting with staffs on a wooden bridge. 'Even when I was making the piece they had not decided where to install it. One suggestion was Nottingham railway station until I pointed out that rival soccer fans would have a field day on the bridge on route to the football grounds, so it was eventually sited in the grounds of Sherwood Forest visitors' centre, the obvious place from the beginning. I selected two earthy characters with tempers to match to be the models. That fitted perfectly in my Barnsley (rough-round-the-edges) version of the confrontation.'

More good news came when he managed to scoop a lucrative hole-in-one. A manager from Center Parcs Holiday Village down the road from the visitors' centre asked him to

'Scales of Justice' … This work represented two styles: the woman has a classical look and the squabbling youngsters are straight out of a comic book. The second image shows details. *Ibbeson Collection*

produce sixteen life-sized statues of the merry band in Lincoln green for a Robin Hood themed golf course.

'I was told only the Hollywood version would suffice. So Errol made a couple of appearances, Maid Marian was a portrait of Carol and I did sneak a couple of my drinking mates in as outlaws. After this project I was asked to sculpt a golden eagle on a tree stump for their new holiday centre in Longleat; my reply was that I did not do eagles. One of the directors laughed and said: "You do". So I did and surprised myself, although it's the friendliest golden eagle you'll ever see.'

Graham once again used his family as models for the three bronze figures unveiled by Arthur Scargill, president of the miners' union, outside the NUM offices in Huddersfield Road in July 1993. There is a minor part of the tableau – dedicated 'in memory of those who have lost their lives in supporting the union and its struggle' – which is disliked by his daughters, that's the dress worn by the figure of the girl. Both Graham and Carol thought the blue dress was pretty when new and worn by the elder daughter, Faye, and later by Emma, but the girls hated it. Emma was used as the model for the girl who

'Fair Maid of Perth' … The fibreglass version now stands at the bottom of his garden, a reminder of a piece of art with a timeless look. *Ibbeson Collection*

represents the 1950s, the decade in which Graham was a child. Carol was again the stoical mother or wife with the babe in arms representing the nineteenth century and there was the late twentieth-century miner. Like some of his earlier work, it has been misinterpreted. People have looked at the barefooted figure of the woman and said that when they were young people wore shoes, but Graham points out she is symbolic of an even earlier age.

The figures represent a number of generations of mining families. Anne Scargill, former wife of Arthur, had a small complaint. She thought the miner's hand touching the shoulder of the girl was not coarse enough for a man who worked underground; Graham replied that the miner was making a gentle gesture at a harrowing time, one that conveyed a softer face of a breed who are habitually portrayed as one dimensional, and in this instance the smoothness of the skin was pertinent.

The councillors in Perth, Scotland were adamant. Yes, they wanted a statue, not in bronze but in fibreglass because it was cheaper. Graham pointed out that vandals would damage anything in fibreglass whereas bronze was far more resilient. 'The Fair Maid of Perth' was based on the title of a Sir Walter Scott story, with Carol as the model. The figure, in medieval costume, is sat on a bench reading one of Scott's books. 'It is about a woman having a rest and contemplating. But there is something mystical, timeless about it. I have a fibre glass version in the garden, see it every day and marvel at its sense of presence.' One day in 1994 Graham, Carol and Max transported the statue in the car to Perth where it was fixed to the appointed bench outside the tourist office. Having spent the night in a B and B, the family walked to the site to discover it had been damaged. 'I did the repairs but told the authorities I would not continue to carry out more if it happened again. It lasted six months before it was damaged once more, this time, they said, by English football fans. By now the authority had changed its mind and wanted the statue cast in bronze. That was in 1995 and it's still there today.'

Rugby School, founded in 1567 and redolent of 'Tom Brown's School Days', is the exact opposite of Cudworth County Secondary School where most of its pupils were methodically shoe-horned into mundane jobs. Rugby is said to be the school where the game of rugby was invented. A group comprising the school, the local authority and the Chamber of Commerce in the Warwickshire town had set up the William Webb Ellis Appeal. It was intended to erect a statue in memory of the boy who is reputed to have picked up a ball during a soccer match while a pupil there in 1823. On entering the sanctum of the senior common room, Graham was 'nervous and felt like a fraud and that I should not be there'. Pictures of the good and the great adorned the panelled walls. He was a whirl of emotions and doubts – he cannot recall what he had for a lunch – but one memory has been retained over the years, the smell of tweed and chalk dust. 'Six of us were shortlisted, I came up with the idea of a boy running with a ball and they liked my approach. I did a maquette, a model of the proposed figure, and took it to the school and that's when I became nervous in the senior staff common room.'

But he won the contract, having demonstrated again that he can transcend his highly nervous interviews in order to get results. There is no likeness of Webb Ellis to be found so he based the 8ft bronze figure on son Max, who was aged thirteen, and added to the image a mop of flowing hair to give the appearance of movement and speed: Ellis, said Graham, must have been running like hell to escape the pursuing public schoolboys. Having completed the fibreglass version, Graham and a pal, Steve Medlam, took it to Rugby and placed it on the plinth to see how it looked. Steve was doing a little rearranging on the figure when a councillor walked up and asked: 'Are you the artist?' Steve replied: 'No, I have got a proper job, I am a mechanic.'

The bronze version was unveiled in the centre of the town in 1998 and this time there was a buffet lunch, at the school. In 2008, a smaller version was produced for the village near Nice in the South of France where Ellis died in 1872. Commissioned by Peugeot, the statue marked the anniversary of his death and the start of the Rugby World Cup in France (the teams were competing for the William Webb Ellis Trophy). Graham was not invited to the ceremony.

'I am proud of the statue but it does look as if it could have been produced 150 years ago. It's got too much grace, it's not earthy enough. I have always been self-critical and often think I could have done better.' The irony of the William Webb Ellis story is that it's never been substantiated, though a famous inscription was cast in stone at the school in 1923 to commemorate his originality. It was not until the 1890s that Rugby School had claimed to be the inventor of the game.

The incredible shrinking woman and another woman who objected to the thought of a little boy flying into her bedroom marked the background to two sculptures in Chesterfield, Derbyshire. The first work was supposed to symbolise the community. The initial candidate on which the work would be based had 'half a Cortina in the garden' and Graham thought he would get a clout (or worse) if his work did not fulfil exaggerated expectations and she was quietly and politely put to one side. The next candidate was successful, a wonderful woman called Kate – the work of art would be entitled 'Kate' – and photographs were taken on which to base the public sculpture. 'When she looked at the photographs she was horrified that she appeared to be so fat and decided to slim. It took eight months to complete the work, during which she lost a third of her weight. When people looked at the statue they thought I had got it wrong. But I hadn't. She had changed and looked different.' Near the housing development

The White Cliffs project … 'The Carousel of Crossings'. *Ibbeson Collection*

'William Webb Ellis' … Graham and Max aged fourteen, with the statue of Ellis who is said to have invented Rugby while at the school. 'He was running like hell after picking up the ball – the entire school must have been chasing him,' said Graham. *Barnsley Chronicle*

The statue outside the school in the centre of Rugby. *Ibbeson Collection*

there was a disused pottery. He had the cast figure dressed in overalls and holding a broken jug with the handle on her lap.

The second public work featured three girls who were concertinaed and a third featured a boy preparing to take off with improvised wings. Positioned on a site in a playground, the statue of the girls was covered in a blue tarpaulin in preparation for the big event. On removing the sheet Graham found they had turned blue. It was lamentably devoid of its natural colour and Graham spent eight hours on cleaning and re-colouring – at least it prepared him for the forthcoming Eric Morecambe statue and Her Majesty the Queen. After the third Chesterfield unveiling – a boy flyer – there was one complaint from a woman who said every morning she opened her curtains to witness a small boy trying to fly into her bedroom.

The Morecambe statue, commissioned by the far-sighted Lancaster City Council, became the most photographed public statue in the North West. As with most public statues the idea took years to bear fruit, mainly because of funding. Graham was delighted to have a go because Eric Morecambe was one of his heroes. The Morecambe and Wise Show in the 1970s was a national institution, particularly at Christmas, and Eric (real name Bartholomew, 1926-1984), had been voted in the UK the most popular comedian of all time. Morecambe was his home town and the idea was that the statue would boost tourist trade, though few people in the early days realised how big it would become.

'It was a dream opportunity but I concentrated too much on my first attempt. I did a portrait and the head was not very good, without character. I had overworked it and there was no depth. I knew I had blown it. It was viewed by Gordon Young, the sculptor, and the team connected with the project, and I could tell from their comments and reactions it was not right. I went to the pub for a few drinks and thought that was it.' On his way home he changed his mind. The following day, working from memories of the television show, he started on a new preliminary model, sculpting in clay, casting in plaster and then painting it. This frenzied burst of energy turned the job around in a day. Then, convinced he had captured the magic of a man who had cast a spell over two generations of television viewers, he transported the model to Lancaster Town Hall. 'I got the job which changed my life. I was told later that had I submitted the original piece I would not have got it.'

At that time there was still a question mark hanging over funding. Despite the hard work of volunteers, various organisations, the council and the *Morecambe Visitor*, the local newspaper, the fund's target was not reached for a total of six years. At times Graham and the organisers wondered whether the statue would materialise. Some donations totalled £10, others £100. There were fund raising gala dinners and other impressive events, but the contract was not clinched until the biggest contributor William Morrisons, the supermarket company, announced a whopping £30,000 gift. The Morrison family, from Bradford, had spent happy holidays at Morecambe when the resort drew enormous numbers of holidaymakers from Lancashire and Yorkshire. Memories of the famous iridescent sunsets on the bay, one of nature's stunning displays, may have been the decisive impulse behind the generous contribution. The project also coincided with the work on the ambitious regeneration of the resort.

Just before Christmas 1998 he was called to Lancaster and told that the funding had been secured. 'That meant work could start on the permanent sculpture which would go on view in Morecambe. I was also told that a special guest would unveil it in July, Her Majesty the Queen. We had been waiting for the total amount of money for six years, now I had six months to do the work and I was really happy, though the panic mode set in.'

On 17 December there was devastating news, another one of those strokes of bad luck that seem to accompany otherwise impressive achievements. Carol was taken ill while wrapping Christmas presents. At first hospital staff thought it was a bug but it turned out to be a brain haemorrhage and she needed pioneering surgery. She survived the haemorrhage and she is all right today, though it was touch and go for a time. 'I had the best and worst news of my life within two days. Carol was in hospital over Christmas and her recovery took a full year, it was a traumatic time.'

Though bewildered and buffeted by events he had an agonisingly difficult decision to make. He had to convince Eric's widow, Joan, and her son Gary, in the February that he had caught the aura of the man and that his version of the 'Sunshine Dance', performed at the end of every TV show, was authentic. Graham described the dance as Morecambe's version of the Highland fling, a confusion of jutting and jostling arms and legs plus a manic grin. He had him dressed in plus-fours and brogues with a pair of binoculars around his neck (Eric was the President-elect of the Royal Society for the Protection of Birds at the time of his death).

Joan and Gary could have been Graham's sternest critics, a minor flaw here or there, a failure to mirror the comedian's charisma and genius, and the project would have been forced back to the drawing board. Joan took one look at the clay version in Graham's studio and announced: 'That's Eric, put the kettle on, Graham.' The glasses, one of the comedian's trademarks, had to be made separately. At the foundry, where the workers were viewing the almost finished bronze figure, one of them said: 'That does not look like Eric.' Graham almost had a heart attack, the perspiration moistened his forehead and he was speechless. Then, with a flamboyant flourish, Ab the foundry owner produced the bronze glasses and put them on Eric's face, declaring: 'It does now.' As soon as the finishing touch was added 'the statue jumped to life'.

'Kate' … The incredible shrinking woman. She had lost so much weight that some people thought Graham had used a different model on which to base the work. *Ibbeson Collection*

'Run, Run Runaway' … Graham tried to 'capture' movement by merging the figures of the three girls. *Ibbeson Collection*

'F F Flyer' … A woman glanced at this statue and thought the boy was trying to fly into a bedroom. One 'boy' was replicated to give the statue a sense of propulsion. *Ibbeson Collection*

Eric Morecambe. *Ibbeson Collection*

TERN MORECAMBE BAY ART PROJECT

You are warmly invited to a reception
in the marquee which marks the take-off of

TERN PHASE II

on Friday 23rd July at 11.00am
at the Eric Morecambe Stage

Prior to this H.M.Queen will be unveiling the Eric Morecambe Statue at 10.00 am

RSVP by 15th July to :
Andrew Clarke, Project Manager,
Lancaster City Council
Town Hall
Dalton Square
Lancaster LA1 1PJ
Tel : 01524 582138
Fax : 01524 582160

The artists involved in the Eric Morecambe Stage are :
Andy Altmann, Russell Coleman, Graham Ibbeson,
Ann Kelly, Shona Kinloch, Jonathan Speirs, Gordon Young

TERN Morecambe Bay Art Project
is supported by :

Arts Council of England
Lancashire County Council
Lancaster City Council
North West Arts Board
Private Donations
Single Regeneration Budget

 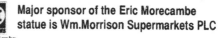

**Major sponsor of the Eric Morecambe
statue is Wm.Morrison Supermarkets PLC**

The invitation to the reception. *Ibbeson Collection*

The foundry owner, putting the finishing touches to Eric. *Ibbeson Collection*

Benny Hill, now at the Club LS1, Leeds. *Ibbeson Collection*

'Some people have said I made Eric and that Eric made me. The work has enhanced my career. But in a way the statue was just the icing on the cake when it comes to the regeneration of Morecambe front. A lot of other artists and craftsmen did a lot of work there to make the area what it is. There were other people who worked hard on that project, all of whom deserve the highest praise. I would have liked to have done a statue of Ernie Wise looking up at Eric and thinking: "He's showing off again", but that was not to be. I sent a letter to Ernie but never got a reply, perhaps he did not get it.'

Not all the projects have happy endings. Eric Morecambe was a resounding success but the Benny Hill statue has had its problems. In 2003 Graham was asked by the nation's favourite TV critic, Garry Bushell, whether he would be interested in doing a life-size statue of the saucy comedian. Nearly ten years later they were still waiting for funding. Graham did, in fact, mould the clay and cast a fibreglass version of Benny as the commissionaire, 'Fred Scuttle'.

At present the figure is on temporary loan to Club LS1, Leeds, where he salutes club members as they enter the premises. But there is a chance the project could be revived.

Chapter 6

Raggy Lads and Les

Carol's prolonged and critical illness and the strain of producing the statue of the UK's best loved comedian took its toll. From 1999 into the spring of 2000 Graham became ill and fell into a scary gloom. 'I felt as if my body was shutting down; all my body ached, I felt exhausted all the time. I was sleeping a lot and could not focus my thoughts.' As Carol recovered – the only sign of the major operation was a dimple on the side of her head where the surgeon had entered to do the brain surgery – Graham suffered physical and mental burn-out. Post-viral debility (like ME) was diagnosed. His reaction to noise became exaggerated. A loud bang would make him shake for ages and the sound of a car horn convinced him the ground was opening up and he was walking on sponge. Even the pub, where the camaraderie helped to relieve the pressures of his craft, lost its lustre.

Anti-depressants and a healthier lifestyle including exercise and a change in diet helped him to emerge out of this personal hell. At the same time he was approached by Leeds Civic Trust to come up with ideas for a public sculpture for the centre of the city. It was a welcome tonic, giving him a new purpose and sense of direction. The local newspaper ran a poll to find the Man of the Millennium and Leeds-born Arthur Louis Aaron, a former student at the Leeds School of Architecture, was chosen. He was twenty-one years old and an acting flight sergeant in the RAF volunteer reserve when he was awarded the VC in the Second World War. His aircraft, a Short Stirling heavy bomber, was hit by gunfire during a raid on Turin in Italy in August 1943. The aircraft was badly damaged, the navigator killed and Aaron's jaw was broken and part of his face torn away. He was given morphine, managed to fly for a while but then gave instructions to the bomb-aimer who successfully belly-landed the plane in North Africa. Aaron died nine hours after the touchdown.

Graham produced a 17ft-high work at the bottom of the Headrow in Leeds on the Eastgate roundabout. It was unveiled in March 2001. 'Although Aaron was a war hero I did not want the sculpture to be a war memorial. I based it on a child's aspirations to fly which Aaron surely had as a child. I needed to design a vertical sculpture so it could be seen on the Eastgate roundabout from all approach roads.'

Leeds pilot Arthur Aaron's statue. *Ibbeson Collection*

Girl releasing dove. *Ibbeson Collection*

Girl with model aircraft. *Ibbeson Collection*

Arthur Aaron in flying jacket is depicted at the base of a tree trunk with four generations climbing the tree. He is shown releasing the hand of the first child, a 1950s boy with bronze (cardboard) wings, catapult in his back pocket and an S-belt. The next generation is represented by a 1970s girl holding aloft a small version of a bulldog in an aeroplane. The 1990s boy handles a model of a space ship and the girl on top – the child of the new millennium – releases a dove. 'I approached the commission with an uncompromising attitude. I actually thought that it may be my swan-song and that I would not have the physical or mental ability to continue with this sculpture malarkey. The result was a very personal piece that happens to be a commission sculpture.' At the base of the tree he had not forgotten a token of the relationship which started in a cafe on the east coast in the late 1960s. 'There is a love heart carved with mine and Carol's initials and the year of our marriage. I am certainly the boy with the cardboard wings stepping up towards the future, my children and grandchildren above me.'

Graham and celebrity Michael Parkinson have at least three things in common. Both went to school in Cudworth (Graham to secondary, Mike to junior), both watched their heroes on the screen at The Rock cinema at Cudworth, and Graham's grandmother and Mike's mother played bingo at The Rock. But, unlike Michael, Graham had little affinity with one of Hollywood's superstars, Cary Grant. Whereas a youthful Michael tried to copy Grant's clipped enunciation and debonair screen character, Graham emulated Laurel and Hardy's antics. Nevertheless he was more than happy to do Grant's public statue for Bristol.

The star's real name was Archibald Alexander Leach (1904-1986). 'This suave, handsome man, one of the coolest guys to stride across the silver screen was being portrayed by this son of a Barnsley miner with an obsession for the portrayal of the absurdities of life.' The statue was unveiled by Cary's widow, Barbara, on a snowy December evening in 2001. The Rock made a lasting impression on Michael Parkinson – in his history of the western the cinema was atmospherically re-created, cigarette ash and all – and on Graham, not just because that's where he watched Flash Gordon and The Three Stooges at children's matinees on Saturdays in the 1950s, but because of the toilets. 'The smell of stale urine will remind me, until the day I die, of my childhood dreams of Hollywood.'

'The Spirit of Jarrow' (the title was selected by the inhabitants) was his next project. As in the case of his mining statues, Graham had more than a passing interest in this venture because some of his mother's family came from the North East. The statue commemorated the 200 marchers who walked from Jarrow to the Palace of Westminster at the peak of The Great Depression (October 1936) to protest against unemployment and the endemic poverty in the North East. The men, led by a firebrand MP, Ellen Wilkinson, lobbied the Government but very little was done and the Prime Minister, Stanley Baldwin, lapsed into economic indolence. However, the march, like Nazi Germany, F D Roosevelt and the talkies, came to symbolise the 1930s, the so-called 'Devil's Decade', and most books covering that period include iconic photographs of the procession marching through villages; newsreels of the grim-faced men and their banner are shown on television today to illustrate that era. The marchers had a bus carrying cooking equipment and ground sheets for when the march had to stop. During the 300-mile march local people often gave them food and shelter. In Barnsley, for example, the men were allowed to use specially heated municipal baths. Many of the men, veterans of the First World War, marched army-style, walking for fifty minutes before having a break and singing to keep up their spirits.

This turned out to be another keenly contested competition between sculptors. As in the Morecambe project lots of help came from Morrisons. The original idea was to have the images of the marchers merged into one block, but Graham changed his mind 'to reflect industry and the community'. He added: 'It was all about a community keeping its belief in itself.' The major industries in Jarrow had been shipbuilding and mining, both of which were devastated by the economic crisis between the wars. His work depicts six life-size figures walking on cobbles, 'Red' Ellen with a babe in her arms (the matriarch of the community), men with flat caps and a seven-year-old girl hand-in-hand with a five-year-old boy who has a toy boat to represent shipping. All the figures are marching out of the ribs of a ship and carry a banner, leaving behind symbols of their crafts – tools and bolts. Graham does not concentrate just on the big picture, he sometimes includes something small but significant in the tableau, a kind of trademark. In the Leeds statue it is a love heart, at Jarrow a Labrador dog, a stray. It's seen on photographs of the march and is said to be have gone to London with the men. The statue received widespread approval: the BBC declared that the 'Jarrow crusade is captured in bronze.' Vince Ray, curator of Jarrow's Viking Gallery, said: 'I think the statue is beautifully cast – it isn't something way out.' The work was unveiled in October 2001, the 65th anniversary of the long march, and among those present was the last survivor, Cornelius Whalen, who ruffled a few historical feathers by telling a BBC reporter 'the march achieved absolutely FA.' He died in 2003, aged ninety-three. Graham, with his acute eye for imagery, believes the work sits comfortably with the rest of his sculptures: 'I felt I was making a monument to a desperate and courageous working-class community. The march south, though futile, was part of my family's heritage. My grandparents come down from that region to Barnsley before the war and my grandmother made sure I knew all about the march.'

A mysterious affliction known as 'railway blight' affected his next project, a problem that had Graham scratching his head until he had a conversation with the technical experts in the pub. He was commissioned by Morrisons to produce three 17ft-wide and 9ft-high stainless steel panels for their car park at a new supermarket at Redcar, Cleveland. He was not all that enthusiastic at first but did some hastily conceived drawings which seemed to find favour with the supermarket chiefs and he went ahead with a two- dimensional project.

His bronze figures of a miner (the area had been known for its iron ore), horses and jockeys (the race course) and an image of a lifeboat (the *Zetland* is the oldest in existence) were superimposed onto the panels. About 50ft of stainless steel was used and the panels were lacquered in different colours. Unfortunately, two months later Graham was told by the architect his work was going rusty. He was gobsmacked. At the pub he mentioned the problem to his pals, Roger and Steve Medlam, who said: 'It's okay, Graham, It's railway blight – we had the same problem at Neddy Green's at

More figures of children. *Ibbeson Collection*

The last survivor of the plane crash, Malcolm Mitchem unveiled the statue in 2001. *Ibbeson Collection*

'Spirit of Jarrow'. *Ibbeson Collection*

'Spirit of Jarrow' outside Morrisons. *Ibbeson Collection*

Redcar, Cleveland: the lifeboat and passers-by. *Ibbeson Collection*

Graham, Tracy Dawson (the widow of Les) and Little Mo, the Mighty Atom, one of Les's friends. *Richard Robakowski*

Graham and the Les Dawson statue. *Max Ibbeson*

Comedian Johnny Vegas with small statue of Les Dawson. *Cornerstone Limited*

Wakefield.' What is railway blight? It transpired the supermarket is near a railway level crossing where trains are stopping and starting all the time, with the result that the braking causes spots of iron and dust to be thrown from the rails and wheels into the atmosphere and onto the panels. Armed with this information Graham, now happy that the trains were culpable and not his workmanship or materials, told the supermarket how to eradicate the blight.

Northern Ireland's first minister and leader of the DUP, Peter Robinson, may still be looking for them. His classy specs, that is. Graham was engaged to produce a bust of the minister. During one of those sessions at which the artist carries out facial measurements he found himself in an awkward position, almost nose-to-nose with Peter, who kept smiling and distracting Graham as he manoeuvred the callipers around his features. Something had to give as each movement of the jaw or lips changed the facial geography: 'Peter, do you mind not smiling?' asked Graham. The reply nearly blew Graham's head off, reminding him of Ian Paisley and his booming voice: 'I am not smiling!' Peter's staff burst into laughter and the atmosphere relaxed. It was not an overnight job and as the work progressed photographs of the bust were sent to Northern Ireland for the minister's perusal.

At that time the politician wore spectacles and Graham did not have a fancy pair to copy, so he used the cheapest (cost: £1). In response Peter, anxious to ensure that his countenance would be portrayed for posterity with all the accuracy of a photograph, sent back an expensive pair which he no longer used. Unfortunately the spectacles were damaged in several mishaps in the studio or foundry: on one occasion a lens fell out, Superglue ended up on the glass during makeshift repairs and then a leg dropped off. 'I think he now wears contact lenses,' said Graham.

Graham sees himself as a kind of Northern comedian. Frank Randle used saucy seaside humour on Blackpool pier shows and Albert Modley from Barnsley convinced audiences he was daft when he drove his tram to 'Duplicate'. Graham uses sculpture to make his audience laugh and his gags are as relevant as any comedian's jokes. Some of his figures, such as his char ladies, have that Norman Evans look about them. Modern comedian Les Dawson modelled one of his routines on the 'Over the Garden Wall' character immortalised by Evans, a comedian from Lancashire, who beguiled holidaymakers and cinema-goers with his version of the toothless middle-aged woman with the rubbery face. Dawson (1931 to 1993) was one of Graham's idols. In 1997, Graham's maquette of the Lancashire comedian was approved by his widow, Tracy, 'but the idea did not get off the ground.' Graham added: 'Everyone loved Les Dawson but we did not know where the funding was going to come from.' In 2007 there was an unexpected development. Graham was told the project was being resurrected and that

The statue at Lytham St Anne's in Lancashire. At the reception the comedian Johnny Vegas, a generous bidder at the charity auction, dropped Graham 'in it' but there were no hard feelings – just laughs. *Ibbeson Collection*

another artist was in line for the job. 'I was on a trip to Blackpool and saw in the hotel a poster advertising the Les Dawson Appeal Benefit Concert. That ruined my weekend.'

Later, Tracy phoned to say a committee had been formed to raise the money for the statue but she was not on the selection panel. It was another uphill battle. He traced the names of the members of the committee and produced a second maquette to prove 'I was the man for the job.' The chairman of the committee, Jim Cadman, had no idea about his previous submission to Tracy. Within nine months the money was raised and in the meantime Graham got the job, basing his statue on the first maquette with a couple of minor refinements.

The statue was unveiled live on mainstream television by Tracy and Les's daughter, Charlotte, in October 2008. A coach load of Graham's pals from Barnsley, known as The Raggy Lads, who have attended some of his other unveilings, turned up at Lytham St Anne's and Graham went with them for a drink in the pub instead of attending the gala dinner after the ceremony. He did not show his face until the auction of items after the meal. The last item was a maquette of Les signed by Graham. When the compere announced that the sculptor was not there because he was down at the pub,

Johnny and Graham after a few pints. *Cornerstone Limited*

comedian Johnny Vegas shouted: 'He's here; he's having a pint with me.' That meant Graham had to go on stage and say something. Unfortunately he isn't accustomed to handling microphones and there was some fumbling and nervousness, at which point the compere said: 'Get the mike closer to your mouth.' There was a pregnant silence among the guests attired in dinner suits and evening dresses when Graham made an inappropriate comment. The silence was followed by a titter in the front row which spread rapidly to the rest of the audience. 'The compere was angry but said later he did not like anyone getting bigger laughs than him.'

Meanwhile, Johnny Vegas, still dawdling at the bar, took over the auction with his customary gusto and crazy humour and bidded against himself for the maquette; it went for £2,000 rather than the last official bid of £1,700. The long wait before the unveiling of the Les Dawson statue exemplified how difficult it is to get such projects off the ground. They are often years in the making. 'People think that being a sculptor is an easy life. Nothing that is any good comes easy. People think that an appeal fund just happens, but there is a lot of hard work involved. It's hard work to do a sculpture, hard work to get the money together and hard to form a committee who can do the fundraising.'

Chapter 7

'Another Fine Mess'

There was a suggestion Laurel and Hardy had stepped down from the big studio in the sky to create anarchy and mayhem. Or maybe Graham's eyes had been moistened by the sight in the workshop of a 12ft-high topless statue of Kate Moss created by the sculptor Marc Quinn. At any rate, Graham found himself unconscious on the ground – knobbled by the heavy hand of fate. While bending down to show the lads in the foundry where to position the dog in the Laurel and Hardy statue, he cracked his head on Oliver's extended hand and fell. 'I had knocked myself out. Coming round I was put on a chair to the sound of laughter. I refused to go to hospital and felt a little unwell on the train back to Yorkshire, but I had survived more unplanned mischief from the comedy duo.'

With the Laurel and Hardy statue, as always, Graham had the last laugh and succeeded spectacularly. It was welcomed by their fan club, 'The Sons of the Desert' (named after one of their feature films in 1933), and unveiled in 2009 in Ulverston, Cumbria, Stan Laurel's home town, amid merriment, an assortment of loonies and the world's press. To cap it all legendary comedian Ken Dodd, who conducted the ceremony, arrived in a Model T Ford.

But the timescale for the statue must have been some kind of record. Graham approached the 'Sons' regarding a memorial in Ulverston in the mid 1980s but never got a reply. In the meantime he did his first Laurel and Hardy figures for a mixed exhibition at the International Garden Festival in Liverpool. 'It was supposed to be around the theme of animals. I do not know how I got away with it but I made a life-size sculpture of them in fibreglass, entitling it 'The Walrus and the Carpenter'. Stan was the carpenter with all his battered tools in his bag, Ollie the walrus. To conform to the animal theme, I put small tusks coming from Ollie's mouth.

'Paul my cousin (6ft 2ins and thin) and me (shorter but chunkier) carried a legend each through the festival site. Both figures had bolts in their feet and the intention was to drill the decking and secure with nuts and washers from underneath. The problem was that the decking was over water and we could not get below to secure. Our solution, in true L and H style, was to put four-inch screws through the fibreglass shoes and into the decking, a bit of a bodged job, but it worked.' Much to the amusement of railway

Laurel and Hardy. *Ibbeson Collection*

workers the comedians were not wrapped when they were sent back to Barnsley and Graham had to collect them from the station.

Graham had always wanted to be one of Laurel and Hardy's pals. 'They did not have the pathos of Chaplin, or the dexterity of Buster Keaton, but what they did have was slapstick camaraderie, warmth and humility, trust and affection, and above all a supreme daftness that followed their silent film days to voices that were perfectly matched to their characters on screen. All this coupled with the genius of Stan Laurel's writing and their perfect timing resulted in a magical combination of visual gags and the inevitable mayhem. That not only shook the rafters of The Rock at Cudworth with laughter but every picture house throughout the world.'

In 1993 a campaign was started to have a memorial to the duo in the town where Stan was born in 1890. Eric Wood, the Grand Sheik of the Behind the Wardrobe Tent of Widnes (each branch of the 'Sons' is known as a tent), took up the challenge and in 2000 Graham was asked to compete for the commission. Among his ideas was the original work from the 1980s, with Stan standing on top of the plinth and Ollie trying to join him on top. Ollie's leg was cocked up as he tried to climb over the plinth and his ample

Graham works on L and H. He removed the wraps on the clay version in his studio every morning and discovered their presence brightened his day. In a similar way their films at the local cinema in the 1950s pepped up his spirits when he was feeling down. *Max Ibbeson*

rear was sticking out. The gag was that Stan's foot was on Ollie's fingers. Graham won the competition but opted for a more affectionate alternative, with the pair leaning on a lamp post with the dog, Laughing Gravy (Hollywood speak for booze).

From the late 1990s Eric and all the 'Sons' raised the money for the statue, on occasions walking into local pubs and singing so loudly the customers paid up to get rid of them. 'Yes, it was a hard slog over nine years, but what fantastic colour my association with these lunatics added to my life. "The Sons of the Desert" raised every penny for the bronze statue, no government grants (though they were offered at the time), no major sponsorship. It was complete dedication. What a set of heroes.'

By 2003 there was enough money for Graham to start modelling in clay: he had helped to boost funds by producing a cast of his scale model and putting the profits from sales back into the fund. 'To add a visual gag I had Laughing Gravy the dog tugging at Ollie's trousers from behind. From the front the boys were smiling for the camera, from the back you saw Ollie trying to shoo away the dog; it was sculpture in the round, visually interesting from all angles.'

Meanwhile the 'Sons' dropped in to see him. On one occasion a mini bus turned up with several lads and lasses, all with fezzes, and singing *We are the Sons of the Desert*. On another a man who had changed his name to T.H.E. Occupier (Thomas Henry Erasmus Occupier) and Mrs Occupier made an extraordinary appearance. 'They had a washing line fixed to the top of the battered estate car to dry their clothes. Ingenious – and very Stan and Ollie – but the road from Huddersfield to Barnsley runs through countryside and their clothes became insect colonies after a fifteen-mile stretch.

'I started to sculpt Stan and Ollie over a winter. It was cold and miserable in the workshop; however, when I took the cover off every morning it uplifted my soul. I set off on the day with a smile. Stan and Ollie were looking down on me with huge grins, and I was looking back at the greatest clowns that have walked this Earth with great affection and joyous memories.'

The money was raised to have the figures cast in bronze in 2005. South Lakes District Council was applying to carry out inner town improvements near Coronation Hall, the perfect site for the boys since Stan and Ollie had appeared on the balcony there during their 1947 visit to this country. Graham received the constant support of Jayne Kendal (of the district council) and Des Metcalfe (landscape designer) and the area was redeveloped by 2009. The statue, which had been in storage in London for four years, was ready to be erected

The night before the unveiling a gala dinner was organised by the 'Sons' at the Coronation Hall to celebrate the end of the long hard years of fundraising: Graham had received his final settlement four weeks before the event. He also received a fillip on being told the dinner would be informal. 'It was a magical, silly night with Ab (the foundry owner) and the foundry lads and lasses, family and friends enjoying the frivolities. I was honoured to receive honorary membership of "The Sons of the Desert": I was a fellow nutcase now.' At one point during the evening Graham turned round to face a posse of L and H lookalikes who wanted his autograph.

On Sunday 19 April 2009, Ken Dodd arrived in the old car driven by the Laurel and Hardy lookalikes and performed the ceremony in front of 2,000, including family, friends and, of course, The Raggy Lads, who are as daft as the 'Sons'. At eighty-one Ken was as amusing as ever. 'He talked affectionately about Stan and Ollie, two great men who had inspired him as a child and whom he saw as comic geniuses. He also paid me a compliment by saying the statues actually looked like the people they are supposed to be. However, to roars of laughter, he accused me of measuring him up for the next job.' Graham's small statue of Ken, produced for his eightieth birthday in 2007, had been presented to him at the Theatre Royal in Wakefield. 'I really felt I had to give something back to a man who has made me laugh from childhood. He thanked me again for the gift on the day of the unveiling.' Graham's wonderful memories of Laurel and Hardy films and Ken Dodd's laughter over the years had made the twenty-five years' wait for the unveiling worthwhile. 'Laurel and Hardy spanned three centuries. They were born in the nineteenth, made us laugh and lifted our spirits in the twentieth and I made the memorial in the twenty-first.' Graham had tried to organise a double unveiling across the Atlantic, via satellite, with one statue in Ulverston and the other in Harlem, Georgia, where Ollie was born, but that never materialised.

The Ulverston statue has captured the warmth and depth of the comedians who dominated cinema screens between the wars. As with many of his statues, the characters look almost animated as if they are about to step off the plinth and walk down the street. The sculpture has mirrored the Eric Morecambe success story because the number of visitors to the Cumbrian town has increased by fifty per cent since the unveiling.

Laurel and Hardy created comical illusions on the screen. A sculptor can create illusions with clay in his studio and this trick of the trade enabled 'Dickie Bird' to change into 'Les Dawson' on the television screen. Once the statue of Dickie, the Test umpire who was born in Barnsley, and who is one of the nation's best loved 'sons', was completed the original clay was used to model Les Dawson. The process was recorded by a BBC time-lapse camera in his studio and screened at the time of the official Dickie Bird unveiling in Barnsley. Sometimes people wonder why statues are not unveiled in chronological order. The Dawson sculpture was unveiled eight months before Dickie's rather than the other way around. The Test umpire's statue was stored in a foundry to wait its turn. 'Sometimes the funding needs to catch up with the progress of the

Ken Dodd with the comedians. *North West Evening Mail*

'The Monster's Frankenstein'. It depicts a monster making Oliver Hardy. The image was inspired by the rail journey made by the two Laurel and Hardy figures produced for an exhibition in Liverpool. They were sent home uncovered in the guards' van to Barnsley railway station where they were a source of amusement until Graham arrived to collect them. *Ibbeson Collection*

Dickie Bird at the unveiling of his statue. Behind him is Phil Coppard, chief executive of Barnsley Borough Council. There were tears of joy when Dickie conducted the ceremony, a few yards from the site of the cottage where he was born. There have been newspaper reports that a copy of the statue may be erected in Australia or India. *Paul Hilton Visual Impact Photography*

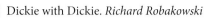
Dickie with Dickie. *Richard Robakowski*

Dickie and Graham with a maquette of the statue. *Visual Impact Photography*

sculpture or there may be problems securing the correct site for the piece, either way it does not always follow that a sculpture that is modelled, moulded and cast into bronze prior to another project starting, is unveiled first. In Dickie's case we had to wait until the site and funding were ready.'

The Barnsley project started when Mel Dyke, a former teacher, brought Graham and Dickie together to discuss a proposal mooted by businessmen who wanted his statue in the town centre. With Mel's help a studio was provided at the local art college where children and students would be able to view the progress of the work. It was hoped that this involvement would give the children a sense of ownership once the statue was erected. The 300 who visited the studio during the two months' work heard Graham talk about his work and Dickie about his days as an umpire. Meanwhile, the BBC TV team put the time lapse camera near the model to record the evolution of the statue.

'The time lapse camera chronicled the modelling and moulding of Dickie and the stripping back of the clay after the process. However the camera kept rolling so the clay I used to create Dickie was the same as I used to sculpt Les. Bird changed into Dawson and it was captured on film. In effect a transition from the 'tears' of Dickie to the laughter of Les.'

Dickie was adamant how he wanted to be portrayed. The finger had to be raised as in the process of sending the batsman to the pavilion and cricket jumpers had to be tied around his waist. The original scale model had the umpire with an expressionless face, after all he was supposed to be impartial at the crease and Graham thought a flicker of a smile could suggest a mildly sadistic streak; but Dickie wanted to smile. 'He was right, his portrait now smiles at motorists and pedestrians in Barnsley town centre.'

There was one unusual feature about this venture. Many of Graham's subjects have not been alive while he's worked on their portraits. 'I had the advantage of live reference, though I was portraying him in his fifties and not as a seventy-six-year-old. I found it difficult not to scrutinise his every movement and facial feature even when we were together socially.'

The statue was erected near to the site of the cottage where Dickie was born (19 April 1933). It was unveiled in June 2009, after which a reception was held at the town hall. Dickie attended the reception but later joined Graham and The Raggy Lads at what became known as the 'uncivic reception' at the local pub, where special free beer tokens were handed to the guests. The alternative event was organised because there were hints that the guest list for the reception at the town hall had been rearranged and Graham's children had not received invitations. This does happen at unveiling ceremonies. At the Eric Morecambe event Graham received his invitation in a brown envelope the day before the ceremony and his wife and children were standing outside the arena

Three photographs of Fred Trueman in clay with Graham. *Ibbeson Collection*

designated for VIPs when Her Majesty the Queen conducted the unveiling. This kind of snub, if that is the correct word, is not just confined to Graham and his family, it is something that is prevalent in the world of art.

Dickie umpired sixty-six Test matches and was made an MBE in 1986. He said at the ceremony: 'I have a few tears in my eyes today. I am very grateful to be here and I am grateful to Barnsley.' He described the statue as marvellous. Cricket fans say it convincingly shows all the characteristics and personality of the umpire who was

Graham and his granddaughter, Poppy, with Fred. *Ibbeson Collection*

admired by the Queen Mother. However, the statue, which is attracting cricket fans in the summer, has an unusual role on Saturday nights – pizzas and items of ladies' underwear have been found hanging from the arm as revellers have wandered around the town centre.*

Dickie was a friend of Fred Trueman, the England fast bowler in the 1950s and 1960s, and a colleague in a powerful Yorkshire cricket team. Fred, a member of a mining family, often gave Dickie a lift in his car after a match and the pair would arrive at the home of Dickie's parents in Barnsley late at night or in the early hours, just as his father was preparing to leave to work in the mine. Fred, the son of a mineworker, felt at home there and stayed for a cup of tea while the conversation revolved around cricket and shift work at the pit.

Working on Fred was Graham's next task. He believes the statue is the most dynamic he has produced, a beautiful study of a great fast bowler in action. Trueman had a sturdy body like that of a miner but ran up to the wicket with the smoothest fluency before releasing the ball at more than 93 mph (92 mph off the pitch). His immaculate bowling action imposed a minimum of strain on his body; he notched up 1,000 overs per season without sustaining the niggling injuries which afflict modern cricketers ('I bowled for twenty years without pulling a muscle,' Fred wrote in his autobiography). Aggression, balance and fluency are encapsulated in the statue.

The Trueman venture started with Graham's close friend, Ashley Jackson, the landscape artist, who in turn was a friend of the former Yorkshire cricketer. At Fred's funeral in July 2006, Ashley mentioned to the bowler's brother Dennis that Graham had said: 'If I did one more portrait before I wobble off this mortal coil I would want it to be the Yorkshire icon and cricketing legend Fred Trueman.'

With the blessing of Fred's widow, Veronica, and the support of Craven District Council and Northern Rail another project was started. It was decided to site the statue in Skipton, Fred's adopted town. Graham's need to find out more about his subject led him to Headingley, Yorkshire County Cricket Club's headquarters, where he was briefed

---

*Dickie is so proud of his statue that during the heavy snow in the winter of 2009 and 2010 he was seen brushing it down to make sure it looked okay. The *Barnsley Chronicle* did not photograph him removing the layers of snow because they thought readers would think it was a publicity stunt which it wasn't of course. If the *Chronicle* had taken the photograph it would have been published all over the cricketing world. Cricket fans elsewhere are not as critical as Barnsley folk.

on Fred's bowling action, and to the Sheffield United Cricket Club where the bowler started his career. The small museum there has a pair of Fred's boots, the right one of which has a steel toe cap. Fred dragged that foot in the final stages of that long run up, something that would not be permitted today. The cap is said to have saved on the cost of footwear but the opposing side sometimes accused him of using the boot to cut up the surface of the pitch near the crease to benefit the bowler at the other end.

'It was an odd and unnerving experience holding Fred's boots. I had the same feeling when I was given the opportunity to hold some of the Viking relics unearthed at the Jorvik dig. My fingers seemed to tingle, I was linked to the people of the past via these objects, and I was responsible for bringing them to life again through my sculpture. What a weight on my shoulders, in fact, the more I thought about it the heavier the objects became.'

It took three and a half years to raise the money. The sculpture was unveiled on 18 March 2010. The initial momentum of the fundraising almost fizzled out after the first two years and nearly halted. 'I felt as though I was the only person pushing the project along. It was hard enough being the sculptor of the project with all the pressures of expectation, never mind having to figure out how to fund the proposal. Veronica was very supportive but we were running out of steam. With the committee's blessing I asked Cornerstone Ltd for help (the same people who enabled the Les Dawson statue to become a reality) and funding was found.'

In a way the long wait was a blessing as it enabled Graham to find out more about the man. Both the maquette and the £90,000 large bronze had Fred in full flow having just released the ball, his right sleeve flapping in the wind. After each delivery he walked back to the start of his run up laboriously rolling up his sleeve to the elbow only to run up to the wicket again with it bobbing and then lolling at his side. It was just one of his little rituals, like using his hand to throw back his mop of black hair or rubbing the new ball on his right thigh or backside. The opposing side had other ideas, claiming this renegade shirt sleeve helped to break the batsman's concentration at the other end. On the maquette, produced three years earlier, Fred had a scowl which did seem appropriate at the time. As in the case of Dickie Bird, this was changed to a flicker of a smile on the larger version. 'This is the most dynamic sculpture I've produced with 500 kg of bronze and Fred moving forward like a raging bull. I felt intimidated by the force of movement, imagining the dread of the recipient of Fred's bowling. I like to think that Fred is looking down (from the Lord's cricket ground in the sky) with a slight smirk and declaring: "Thas not done bad, lad, it's bart time I had a statue, a deserve it".'

Fred (his Yorkshire career started in 1949 and finished in 1968) was the first to attain more than 300 Test wickets and Herbert Sutcliffe, the Yorkshire and England batsman,

Bowling was always hard work for Fred during his 'pomp' in the 1950s and 1960s. Graham paid tribute to all that sweat, a sign of honest toil, when he mopped the brow of the fast bowler at the unveiling ceremony. *Cornerstones Limited*

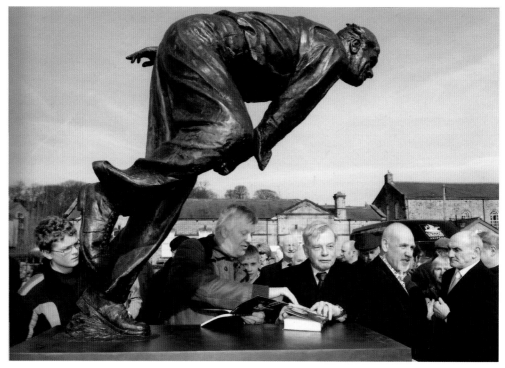

Graham and Dickie at the Fred Trueman unveiling. Cornerstones Limited

said statistics suggested he was the best bowler of all time. Asked whether the then record would be broken, Fred said: 'Perhaps but he'll be bloody tired.'

Phil Tregoning, writing in the magazine *Art of England*, described the statue as 'a masterful piece of sculpture now proudly towering over the market square of Skipton. The sculptor, Graham Ibbeson, creator of this fine figure in flannels, appears to have given the townsfolk of Skipton exactly what they want, as opposed to the plethora of "if you do not want what I want, then you are narrow-minded" oddities that have little to do with the public and much to do with making the reputations of artists and curators.'

Tregoning believes public art is following the same shaky path as the present school system – 'the kids have stopped listening'. But more work like Graham's will help to reverse that trend, he believes.

Chapter 8

Angel Delight

Graham recalls his miserable little Angel with affection. She helped to change his approach to work when moving from fibre glass to metal while he was experimenting with ideas. The Angel was an 18 inch-high bronze figure of a little girl with pitiable eyes who is descending a flight of stairs with a suitcase in one hand and a carrier bag in the other. The bottom lip 'is curled down with an inevitable look of resignation,' personifying domestic dejection and rejection.

He knew his gamble in bronze had paid off when he walked into the Lunts' foundry in Birmingham: there is always a friendly welcome, but this time it was different as the new figure had produced smiles and laughter all around. He had captured the kind of transitory expression which only a child can produce and which is recalled with pleasure years later by parents and grandparents. 'The response was fantastic. The delivery of the narrative and humour worked just as well in metal.' (There is another happier version of the Angel walking back up the steps).

In about 2000 he started to cast his fine art work in bronze again as well as in fibreglass. It was not easy. He had to pay for the bronze casting – with his public sculptures the bill was met by the people behind the commission – and manhandling bronze was heavy work. You can lift a 3ft-high fibre glass figure with one hand; a similar sized bronze figure takes two men. Another aspect is that the sculptor has to relinquish some control over his work when the figure is handed over for casting and in addition the process is slower than working in fibreglass.

Nicholas Treadwell, the art dealer, who was exhibiting Graham's highly coloured fibre glass figures at the time, said he did not want to show what he called 'brown art' (bronze work) at his gallery as he believed it was old fashioned. 'I suppose he thought I was harking back to the nineteenth century. Of course I completely ignored the advice and took the bull by the horns and produced a couple of bronze pieces. The irony of it all was, by casting my work into bronze, I was elevating it to "high art" status, thus taking the joke a step further.'

In this new experimental period he did not change his attitude towards humanity, humour, form, rhythm or shape. The new work was a mere expansion of his style. 'The forms had to be stronger and the modelling sharper to compensate for the lack of colour. You can patinate the surface of bronze in many colours by using different chemical applications and even paint the surface. I opted for the more traditional approach of brown and greens.'

Phil Tregoning, of Tregoning Fine Art, Derby, who had shown Graham's fibreglass work in the past, encouraged him to continue casting in bronze and exhibited his new work. Most of his small bronzes are in editions of nine and until the present day Phil has sold at least one of every edition. Nicholas Treadwell had to eat his words and exhibited his work as well. 'The thing is that my commissioned work, initially undertaken to subsidise my fine art work, taught me to adapt my sculptural approach in modelling for bronze.'

His bronzes included not just an Angel but another visually stimulating work with vaguely religious overtones, the Barnsley Buddha. The piece was influenced by what he saw in the Far East (the bronze Buddha figures in temples and hotels, for example) and by the old Barnsley dialect. Again it had a flying theme. He sculpted the head and shoulders of an Angel with wings, flying cap and goggles and medals on the chest and with the shape of a screw forming the point at the peak of his helmet.

To try to describe some of his figures does not do them justice. The Barnsley Buddha is one example. The description seems bizarre but Graham has a careful eye and is a consummate visual artist; take a look at one of the models and any doubts or reservations about his work are summarily dismissed. The Buddha was what he called 'a post-industrial god watching over Joe Public.' The title, 'The Little Barnsley Buddha', originated in the days when some mothers in Barnsley shouted 'Come here you little bugger' (it sounded like Buddha even to the initiated).

For years he had been wondering how to produce a bronze work based on the rhyme 'sugar and spice and all things nice.' The answer to his prayers came when he spotted an old mincing machine in a pal's farmhouse. 'The main body of the machine I sculpted took the form of a pregnant woman. There was a handle to turn at the back. The idea was that sugar and spice with puppy dogs' tails went in the top, you turned the handle and babies were produced. Of course the machine did not actually work, though there were about twenty pewter babies scattered around the base and one was flying out of the funnel at the front. Again I was not bothered about the mechanics of it all just the visual possibilities – the same attitude I had as a kid.'

The piece received a verbal drumming from a pregnant woman who attended its first viewing at a gallery in Austria. 'The German said she did not like it, declaring that only a man could make it. I said that surely such a machine, if it was possible to make one work, made men redundant; she in turn said it was probably a man who was turning

'Down to Earth' which highlighted new aspects of his work. *Ibbeson Collection*

Head of a Barnsley Buddha. Graham was fascinated by the sight of figures while touring in the Far East. This one has a Barnsley flavour. *Max Ibbeson*

the handle. Her English was excellent and her expletives very precise. The rhyme was lost in translation.'

On occasions Graham has done work on a whim. He went to the foundry to inspect one such piece, a tower of seven babies in foetal positions. A foundry lad asked: 'What's all this about, Ibbo?' to which he replied: 'I have no ruddy idea at all.' (The same answer he gave the tutor at Leicester Polytechnic all those years ago). The lad laughed but Graham said it was basically true. To make things worse he had spent a considerable amount of money on what turned out to be a whim. 'Sometimes I have clear cut reasons for making a particular sculpture; at other times I see an image that I want to elaborate upon and follow my instincts. A good friend Baz Cross told me about an art lesson he had as a kid. The class was asked to draw animals and Baz came up with a crocodile with wheels instead of legs. The puzzled teacher questioned the decision to use wheels. The reply: "Cos I can't do legs, Sir". A clip round the head was given rather than praise for inventiveness.'

'Freddy Neptune' … a boy with a model of a galleon on his head. He has become the family's coat of arms. 'He looks confused and the family felt sorry for him, so they adopted him,' said Graham. The family has named a new company after this character. It handles all requests for images of the artist's work including prints and posters. The idea to create a company came after Graham appeared on the popular television programme Flog It, after which he was inundated with phone calls regarding his work. Many of the callers asked where they could get copies and images of his work. *Freddy Neptune Limited*

'Vending Venus' … the baby-making machine which upset a pregnant visitor to a gallery in Austria. *Max Ibbeson*

His granddaughter Poppy, born at the beginning of 2004, has inspired him to produce new ideas. He had made several bronze statues using babies in previous years 'but now the inspiration came from the objects that come with having little ones around, in particular the teats for babies' bottles.' He placed a baby modelled in a foetal position on top of a 3ft sculptural form representing a rocket and then placed baby's teats all over the rocket, cast in bronze and entitled it 'Mothering Ship'.

Graham has always wanted to produce paintings to accompany his sculptures, but a blank piece of paper and colour constricts him. Give him a pencil and he'll skilfully produce a sketch as per the

This intriguing piece was entitled 'Compact Colin'. *Freddy Neptune Limited*

'Mothering Ship' … This work depicts a baby on a rocket covered in teats. He got the inspiration from all the paraphernalia parents buy when there is a new arrival in the house – in this case teats. Poppy, his beloved granddaughter, not only changed his style but his life. *Ibbeson Collection*

excellent collection with the British Council; however, paint and paper do not mix well in his world. In the 1980s he was asked by a publisher to produce a series of colour illustrations for a book based on 'The Grimethorpe Flyer'. He could not come to terms with using paint on white paper and the project was dropped, though he did suggest using photographs of his 'flyer' in the book.

Drawing has proved to be a durable and satisfying alternative to painting. It was his second love. His first was pop music but any ambition he had to be a rock star was smashed – literally – and as a result drawing became his predominant skill at school. This critical change in his life started after he had saved enough money from his paper round to buy a guitar and Bert Weedon's 'Play in a Day' book of lessons. While Graham was practising in the living room, his father, who was watching the evening news on

A charcoal drawing of boy with a colander on his head. It's an everyday scene from childhood, though most adults would deny that it ever happened to them. *Freddy Neptune Limited*

Pencil drawing of a boy whose wings are beating so fast he looks as if he is flying. *Ibbeson Collection*

Boy with tomahawk, a 1982 pencil drawing. Violence is an underlying theme in his work. He points out there is nothing more violent than a 'Tom and Jerry' cartoon but few people object to their anarchy and mayhem. This work was based on the incident when Graham was injured while playing as a youngster. *Freddy Neptune Limited*

Portrait of Poppy, his granddaughter, as the 'Grimethorpe Flyer'. An example of his preoccupation with flight, escape and childhood memories. *Freddy Neptune Limited*

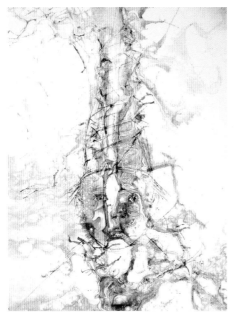

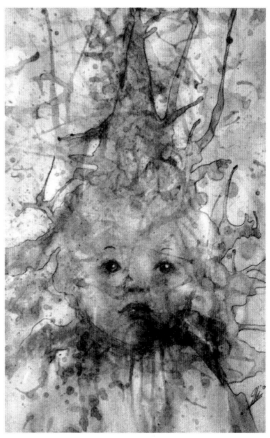

Faces in Flames … a baby's face in paint. Sculpting is all about discipline, firm lines and images worked out in advance. At other times he indulges in a form of painting which relies on indiscriminate and liberal use of paint and an imagination which produces a face out of a chaotic mixture of colour. Graham splashes paint on a sheet of paper and then looks for images which can be turned, with the aid of a pencil, wax or charcoal, into faces. *Freddy Neptune Limited*

Another Little God. *Freddy Neptune Limited*

television, asked him to stop. Graham continued and father told him to pack it in. His mum gave Graham a gentle warning and then his father shouted: 'Graham bloody be told.' There was no response from the strumming guitar man who was dreamily emulating Bert or one of the more fashionable pop stars; his father jumped out of his chair and smashed the instrument on the fireplace. 'The sound it made was more tuneful than any of my attempts to master the instrument.' The following week his father bought him a second-hand guitar but by that time he had set his sights elsewhere.

Instead he turned to drawing. As teenagers he and a mate used pencils to copy a photograph of Paul McCartney. His pal, who later became a draughtsman, took methodical measurements of the facial features while Graham took one look at the image and used his instincts to produce the best reproduction. Even in childhood influences came from unusual places. His father had smashed the guitar on the fireplace

'Grimethorpe Flyer Third Attempt' (1979) … The boy is on the point of being propelled into space with the aid of a rocket and cardboard wings. *Freddy Neptune Limited*

but a friend's father used their fireplace to illustrate skills in drawing, an exercise in craftsmanship which impressed Graham. His first friend was Ronnie Neville, now a photographer. Ronnie's father, Ivor, a miner, was a character who indulged in his passion for untutored sign writing by artfully covering Danny Oates' ice cream vans which were known to almost every child in Barnsley. Many of the National Coal Board signs at pits in Barnsley were produced by Ivor.

Graham was sat in their room when Ivor started to draw with pencil on the ceramic tiles on the fireplace. 'It was magical; out of his head he produced a photo-like image of the head of Jesus with a crown of thorns. He had just completed it when Phyllis (Ronnie's mother) entered and accused Ivor of mucking the house up and with one wipe of the dish cloth the masterpiece disappeared as if by the hand of God. Ivor shrugged his shoulders and went down to the Albert Club. Everyone listened to Ivor when it came to art.' Graham recalls that sometimes Ivor asked his wife whether she had seen any of his paintings. 'They are all over the place and I used one to light the fire,' she would declare. Many miners had hidden talents, including Graham's father who was capable of skilfully constructing a miniature play house for children, and Ivor was another who did not reach his potential. In some respects they were members of a lost generation, having been born at the wrong time and in the wrong place.

Graham has been drawing for fifty years and the British Council bought a collection of his work thirty years ago including a series of images chronicling the life of 'The Grimethorpe flyer' ('All artists take the same route, they never get to the stage of becoming an adult'). The drawings were bought as a result of one of his exhibitions in London, after which the The Sunday Times enthused about his work while The Guardian came to a more basic conclusion, claiming he was an artist who indulged in artistic self abuse. Most people would see them as wonderfully crafted images of ridiculousness which display both the talent of a draughtsman and the wizardry of a cartoonist. None of the sketches is excessively imaged. One shows an incipient aviator trying to take off with cardboard wings which are beating so quickly he seems to have become a human dragonfly; the others depict a boy or girl trying to reach for the sky in what look like hastily converted prams or television sets with a single propeller to whiz them into the unknown. These images have a passing reference to Heath Robinson inventions and all were strikingly innovative at the time.

The sketch books which he has kept since 1967, complete with small drawings, trace his creative path. He seldom does detailed drawings of a proposed sculpture, relying instead on quick sketchbook ideas and notes before starting in clay and using photographs and models for additional reference. 'Carol danced on one leg so I could get the folds and action right on Eric Morecambe and she was the action model for comedian Benny Hill (which was to be sited in Southampton), Laurel and Hardy and the stainless steel nativity scene for Barnsley (she was the Three Wise Men, Joseph and the Virgin Mary and many more, poor lass).'

His acceptance to Barnsley Art School in the 1960s was based on his ability to draw. However good he was, it did not mean he was an artist. Now he realises that that skill comes down the list. 'To me the essential element is imagination, coupled with a sense of play and understanding of the visual language. Skill and creative thinking need to be married to form true artist expression. I have lost count of the people who have said they have a child who is an artist. No; they are not, they can draw and most children can. It's instinctive. They make creative marks on paper trying to portray and make sense of the fascinating new world they have been born into. Learning to write comes much later. You have to earn your artistic stripes.'

He earned his stripes at the Chesterfield Art College. The Polish tutor, a teddy bear of a man, having seen something special in his drawings, suggested he should rearrange his priorities and concentrate on sculpture, pointing out that he had an understanding of shape and form. The tutor taught him the rudiments of sculpting over a month or so, during which Graham said 'a light had been turned on and his path had been illuminated'. Even today drawing has its advantages. Working on a piece of sculpture and waiting for someone to raise the money is a slow process – it can take a year from the initial idea to reality, twenty-five years in the case of Laurel and Hardy – so his first artistic love provides an instant creative release. At his solo exhibitions he shows his drawings in their own right. His gag drawings (not his preparatory work for sculptures) are usually in pencil and the large charcoal ones are a mixture of what he calls one liners and portrait studies.

'Recently I have taken them a step further by using colour. I have no qualms about using colour on my sculptural work as on some occasions paint brings the work to life; however, I seldom use colour on a flat surface. It all changed when I attended a mono print course (mono print is a process of applying paint to glass and taking one print off). I originally went to make the numbers up and came away with a completely different attitude to my two dimensional work. The thing that inspired me most was not the process but the feeling of freedom. You were working intuitively in a spontaneous way. It also occurred to me that when painting I was intimidated by the white expanse of paper, so an arbitrary application of colour on the paper to break up the surface put me at ease.'

Having splashed paint freely and indiscriminately over the paper, he goes to work looking for random images on the surface as children had done when peering into coal fires in the past, after which he uses a pencil, crayon or charcoal to emphasise and

'Ophelia 90', the wall relief. *Ibbeson Collection*

'Knife Thrower's Assistants' … A darkly comical image with Carol as the mum who is blissfully unaware of the impending danger as she poses for a gentle family portrait. The boy, who is alert to what is happening around him, is about to leap out of the picture frame to avoid the flying hatchets, leaving Mum to her own fate. *Ibbeson Collection*

'Something has Come Between Us' Is it the baby? *Freddy Neptune Limited*

The cross at the Emmanuel Church in Barnsley. The piece was prompted by the simple image of a slither of light projected by a street lamp into the bedroom. *Ibbeson Collection*

'Down to Earth' … the classical version. The downcast Angel, alias granddaughter Poppy, aged six, is seen with a supermarket plastic carrier bag full of her belongings. This is said to be a modern version of the self portrait of Graham at the bus stop; this time, however, the main figure is Poppy who is seen walking away from home. Not that his granddaughter has contemplated running away from home. *Freddy Neptune Limited*

highlight the outlines of his new found shapes, which are usually similar in appearance to children's features. This ongoing series is entitled 'Little Gods' (Little Buddhas).

His other love: 'wall reliefs'. His work, 'Ophelia '90', is a reference to the 'Ophelia' (1851–1852) by the great Pre-Raphaelite painter Sir John Everett Millais. Ophelia, a character in Shakespeare's 'Hamlet', is seen floating down the river before she drowns. It is now seen as a thing of beauty which praises the features of the landscape. Graham has adopted a modern theme for his work, a comment on world pollution. 'My version shows a life-size woman (Carol), floating down a river on a bed of junk, some of it relics from childhood, pram wheels, toy space gun, a seaside bucket and some of my mother's jewellery. Ophelia's demise is brought about by the pollution of life, not by the grief and the loss of life as in the original version. She held a spanner in her hand (a symbol of technology) in my first version, but I have now updated that version and she holds a mobile phone instead.'

With a wall relief he uses shadow to create depth and what he calls the illusion of form through perspective. 'I have used certain tricks to make my figures look whole, to have them coming out of a wall or frame. One of my fibre glass wall reliefs showed a group of men looking out of a bar window and admiring a young lady walking by. It included a publican, several builders and businessmen. In another work I portrayed Charlie (his father-in-law) looking lovingly at his wife, bunch of flowers in his hand, and silly grin (he had been to the pub and his amorous advances are welcomed by his missus). Another relief depicted a husband and wife in bed, patchwork quilt pulled up to their chins, not a chance of getting any sleep with the baby sat up in the middle shrieking its little head off. It was entitled "Something's Come Between Us".'

His large wall reliefs have been commissioned by companies. A five by five metre wall relief was undertaken for a shopping centre in Putney, London. Showing two boys putting giant jigsaw puzzles together, it was secured to the side of the building for a projected three month period because the opening of the building had been delayed. It stayed for three years, long after the opening, the owners having discovered the shoppers liked it.

Commissioned by a building society office in Barnsley, one of his favourite wall reliefs depicts the profile of a family group who appear to be moving boldly into the future and away from the pits and glassworks in Barnsley, the worn out industries. All three of his children and his grandson, Jordan Abraham, feature in the tableau which is so life-like the figures appear to be on the verge of bursting into life and making their way towards the reception area. All the faces have the granite-like determination that you sometimes see in that pugnacious but bewitching art produced by the Soviet Union between the wars. There is a sense the past has long gone and that the town is moving forward. He

painted it with flesh tones, toned it down with a black wash and then varnished it to darken the colour, giving the figures the sense that they are on the move.

In 2003 he produced a wall relief for the local church. As so often before he can have a clear reason for making a sculpture or inspiration can come from all kinds of things – even a thin band of light thrown by a street lamp into the bedroom. He had a flash of creativity which turned out to be prophetic and which reminded him of the dream about the eagle and cherub in the foundry. He's not particularly religious but this incident set him thinking. During a restless night he was looking at a gap in the curtains – they had not been drawn properly – and the middle section of the window appeared to form a cross as the yellow light beamed in. Within a couple of weeks he was approached by the newly opened Emmanuel Methodist Church in Barnsley – would he be interested in designing a cross for them? The 10ft-high stainless steel cross was in place by Easter 2003, a jagged sliver of golden or yellow light radiating from it.

'That was another odd incident in a very odd career...'

Chapter 9

'Uphill Struggle'

Graham's mental fuses were almost blown by a scene which electrified his senses in a park near Oslo in Norway about five years ago. The Vigeland Sculpture Park, covering 80 acres, has 212 separate sculptures in bronze, stone and wrought iron, the work of the most prolific sculptor the world has known. Gustav Vigeland (1869–1943) created it between 1907 and 1942. The centrepiece is a 57ft elaborately evolved carved block of granite (The Monolith), with 121 over life-sized naked figures of men and women and children, a sight which Graham found to be 'awe inspiring'.

A chance conversation with a lover of art, a former sailor, sent Graham and Carol off on a trip to Oslo to learn more about this wondrous and mysterious world which had transfixed his pal. Graham has seen and appreciated all kinds of art from all over the world but nothing prepared him for Oslo. On entering the park he was in an ecstasy, a kind of trance. 'As a sculptor I visually could not take in the image at first, my eyes were darting all over the place and my brain could not decipher the information. The only other time I have had this kind of sensation was climbing the steps of Barcelona's underground station to confront the vision of the Gothic Cathedral. On both occasions I thought I was going mad and was in a parallel world that I could not comprehend. It took only a few seconds for my brain to adjust, but it was an experience that still haunts me, utter confusion.

'The work shows all aspects of the human condition, family life and community, with all the frailty and strengths. It has humour, tenderness, grief and compassion. It conveys the life and spirit of humanity. In other words it was the wheel of life – which is the title of one of the sculptures.'

The UK does not treat its artists very well, so what happens abroad can take us by surprise. For instance, in the 1920s Oslo built a mansion for Vigeland to use as a studio and dwelling. It was returned to the city on his death and became a museum. It houses 1,600 sculptures and thousands of drawings and prints.

'The museum was the most fascinating place I have ever visited. His motivation and his working processes were laid bare. We were there quite early in the day and still there at closing time late in the afternoon. Just before the museum closed we were asked by

'Seven Sons' … inspired by Vigeland. Ibbeson Collection

Vigeland, the sculpture park which left Graham entranced. The style of sculpting had parallels with Graham's work. Yet he had never heard of the Norwegian sculptor until he met a former sailor. *Ibbeson Collection*

one of the attendants if we would like to see Vigeland's personal quarters. It may be they were so receptive because we showed such an interest in the mechanics of it all, they can't get many people enthusing so much about plaster moulds. His private area was tiny with a cot bed and viewing balcony so he could see his work below and his hat and coat were hung on the door. What I found very strange on seeing his sensitivity as a sculptor and his depiction of humanity, is that there was no reference to his family. In contrast, Carol has accompanied me through the ups and downs of this precarious profession and has been one of my models throughout my career.'

Yet Graham had never heard of the sculpture park or its creator until he met one of the Raggy Lads, Jack Brown, who had been there when he was on shore leave from the Royal Navy in 1955. Graham met Jack after a committee was formed in 2002 to discuss the sculptural proposals for an empty plinth in the centre of Barnsley. Graham's proposal for 'a tower of people', a vertical community, was reminiscent of Vigeland's 'column of life', said Jack. The former teacher, who loves the arts, went on to speak buoyantly and comprehensively about the Norwegian sculptor. The allure of the park proved too much for Graham who thought he had found the work of a kindred spirit. 'Carol and I collected our air miles and went to Oslo. If I had made the trip twenty-five years previously, it would have changed the course of my work. I had fought for years to get recognition of my type of work and it was validated on a weekend in Oslo. My concerns are different today, however.'

He added: 'By the way, I sent Jack a photograph of me next to the Monolith. He was appalled when I told him it was £9 for a pint of beer in Oslo.'

There was another surprise in Norway. The females represented in the Vigeland sculptures appeared to be strong characters, just as they were in the old mining communities. Graham says strong women 'hold the fabric of a community together with compassion, determination and unfaltering inner strength, virtues that manifested themselves in my childhood and in the women of the mining community in the 1980s'. His work has always portrayed women as a dominant force in a relationship.

'As a child I saw it in my mother and in all the women around me, an unflinching belief in the family unit with a determination to protect their family and offspring coupled with the stamina to do it day in and day out. I also saw it in my grandmothers. My paternal grandmother, Elsie, raised a family of four with the use of only one arm, the other having been paralysed when she was a girl.'

This type of woman features in his work. In 'The Spirit of Jarrow' the firebrand and dimunitive MP, 'Red Ellen', is the first to march forward. 'The Scales of Justice' shows the strength and impartiality of a mother. 'The Coal Queen' and 'Redundant Fairy', ironically, spotlight the demise of two male dominated industries and the miner's widow, part of

'Uphill Struggle' … His close observations of mothers on shopping trips and engaged on household chores has proved to be a fruitful and enduring source of creativity for Graham. *Ibbeson Collection*

'Pressing for Pleasure' … a woman irons her oversized knickers, another of Graham's crazy creations. *Ibbeson Collection*

the Jim MacFarlane Memorial Sculpture, shows a proud figure in a defiant stance, 'the true spirit of a mining community'.

His mother was a strong character. As mentioned earlier she was determined to get a bungalow and despite having been in hospital following an angina attack she went and bought one in a neighbouring village, though she spent only a few days in her dream home before she died. Such strong-willed women can be seen in the novels of D H Lawrence, the son of a Nottinghamshire miner who chronicled life in pit villages in the early years of the twentieth century. His women seemed to remain remarkably intact and in charge even after their husbands and the rest of the community were coming apart in the midst of a crisis such as a strike or mining disaster. During the 1984/85 miners' strike women played an important part in supporting the union, and it was not just a case of running soup kitchens.

In his fine art work he has taken a more sideways look at women. 'Uphill Struggle' (now on display in the Barnsley Development Agency Offices at Westgate Plaza) features the unenviable side of a mother's life, a woman pushing a pram burdened with shopping up a hill; there are tracks in the ground left by the wheels of other prams. Her child is sat upright in the pram, smiling and sure of his mother's love but oblivious to the effort undertaken by her on the difficult route home. 'Woman Flattens Husband after he comes home from the Pub' and 'A Wife on the Ocean Wave' are not only funny but emphasise his view women are not the weaker sex. 'Pressing for Pleasure', a life-sized sculpture of a woman who uses the steam iron attached to her feet to press her oversized knickers, is said to personify a woman's ingenuity, and 'Zoo Keeper at the Female Enclosure' is darkly comical and elusive and shows that women can wield power and manipulate love or male fear even when they are incarcerated: a desperate zoo attendant is seen having to ward off the inhabitants of the female compound. 'The women are not seen in the piece but their presence is suggested by the lipstick imprints on the frightened man's face and the huge pair of bras thrown over his head by the captives.'

The woman who features in most in his work and who has been one of his models since the early days is Carol, whose likeness can be seen in statues all over the country. He sees her as having a strong character, the lynchpin of the family, who evaluates his work and whose physical fitness has been jeopardised by his vocation. On his return to full-time education in 1971 – he was not entitled to a grant until he went on a degree course – Carol worked in a sewing factory for a year to keep the family afloat.

'Times were hard. We both worked hard to keep the dream afloat. I would have faltered way down the line without Carol's constant support and her unquestioning belief in me as an artist. From leaving college I have nearly always worked from home, in a workshop, shed or even carport behind the house. Carol has been constantly on hand, my assistant, muse, and probably my most honest critic, the first person I call upon to view a piece in progress to pass critical comment. What rows have erupted from these discussions. It's never stopped her telling the truth though. We have stood side by side working on some of the sculptures for weeks, rubbing down car body filler to hide the seams on the fibreglass work, resulting in Carol getting calluses on her hands and in having steroid injections in her elbow joints.

'She has also been my constant reference point for the female form and her features can be seen in many of my sculptures and two-dimensional works. This has kept down the cost to an absolute minimum by not paying for a model; it also endorses that endearing Yorkshire trait of being a tight-fisted so-and-so. Carol does not grumble any more about being called upon to model. She is getting on a bit and my portraits always show her as a twenty-five-year-old.'

The couple moved to Ripley after their wedding and bought their first house in 1970 for £850 and upgraded in 1971 to a house costing £950. They were still paying the mortgage when Carol's mum and dad bought it. The proceeds were used as a deposit for a house in Barnsley when he left the Royal College. The decision to abandon London, the centre of the art world, seemed to many to be a backward move but not to the family. 'We loved London, the access to museums and galleries, the buzz of the capital. But on leaving college I became a member of the real world again and that meant Barnsley. I have exhibited my Barnsley creations all over the world and have been called upon to undertake public sculptures throughout the UK without being surrounded by the pretentiousness that is part and parcel of the arts system. I have friends who are artists, musicians and writers, and I hold them dearly. They mostly have the same motivation and attitude as me towards their creative undertakings. To me an artist must be true to his or herself, the problem is some artists are more honest than others.'

He is neither working class nor middle class but when he lived in a detached house in Doncaster Road, Barnsley, he was shocked during an election to discover that children had thrown stones at his property because they thought owners of largish houses did not vote Labour. Having pursued one of the boys down the street, he found himself facing the formidable and threatening mother, an example of Yorkshire's strong-willed women, the backbone of much of his work, and backed off.

Carol believes she is married to an obsessive. She said: 'I am always having a go at him; he does not listen. It's the downside to working from home and to being an artist. The other downside is the mess that is created by making sculptures. It cannot be contained in the workshop and it's way down Graham's list of priorities. Our marriage has been a bit of a rollercoaster – interesting, stressful and colourful in equal parts. We met when we were mere kids and moved into adulthood together. I am proud of his achievements.

'Zookeeper at the Female Enclosure' … *Freddy Neptune Limited*

One of Graham's strong female images. The 'Coal Queen' was destined for a former colliery spoil heap, a kind of 'Angel of the North' but the project never materialised. *Ibbeson Collection*

I know the hard work that goes into each piece and the sacrifices he has made over the years.'

Another woman with a strong character in the family is 'Ar Ugly, Gail', who was frequently tormented by Graham when younger but who has become feisty. She was born four days before his third birthday. While his mother was heavily pregnant she was taking Graham to Leeds but the trip was cut short when she fell on Cudworth railway station. 'I could not understand what all the fuss was about and I did not get my ride on a steam train.'

One incident from their childhood sticks in his mind. He was sitting at the back door and Gail came running down the garden, tripped and knocked out a row of top teeth and most of her bottom. 'I ran to tell my mother but our paths crossed because she had heard the screams. I kept shouting: "It's not me"; "It's not me" and hid in the cupboard under the stairs. It was mostly me who made her scream as a child. I tormented her something rotten to get a reaction.

'I think the genes she inherited from my grandmother and the taunts she must have had from looking different after she fell down built her strength of character. She was not going to be shoved around and put on.'

Graham says outwardly she's not scared of anybody or anything. She has defended her family, her brother and friends 'verbally and occasionally physically' and 'treads fearlessly where tough and muscular men would have second thoughts'.

She can read a situation and sort it out immediately 'probably not the way I would have approached the problem but with better results'. Yet she is a mother hen who is sensitive and thoughtful, protecting her brood while reacting against bullying and injustice. 'She is now fighting her way back from illness and she's winning. I knew she always would.'

It's also got to be said that Graham's affability and congeniality conceal a steel bar inside him and that his character is as strong as any of the formidable women in his family; he is a man who has come to the conclusion that what does not destroy him makes him stronger. Eschewing the easy way in life, he made a number of difficult decisions when he was young by turning his back on a grindingly predictable job at the National Coal Board workshops and then by getting out of his suffocating but familiar environment. Like one of his miners in a pit memorial who 'fights' the coal with his pick, he has had to battle in his own way to be accepted; there was no featherbed of privilege or qualifications on which to start his career, and he has accomplished it without losing his sense of humour. He has found himself in uncharted waters with no manual with which to navigate an orderly course in life, though his parents gave him lots of assistance at art school and his father's younger brother, Len and his wife, Doreen, still encourage him by attending exhibitions and unveilings. Also he has brought up a family whilst working in an unpredictable occupation, and living in a town which is not stuffed with like-minded artists.

Other work encroaches on his sculpting. A substantial slice of his life is taken up with all the backroom stuff; there are lengthy meetings and long discussions with the people who have commissioned his work and who can be hypercritical, hesitant, delighted or exuberant when they see the preliminary drawings or the clay model for the first time. He can recall his angst before the Morecambe family arrived in Barnsley to view Eric's statue for the first time, at a time when Carol was very ill in bed. Luckily there wasn't a problem and the family went away without a flicker of disapproval. He also has to work out prices while simultaneously marketing and promoting his sculptures and looking after the business side.

Sometimes he has to pay scrupulous attention to countless details, more the responsibility of a manager or PR than a sculptor. The public has a preconceived notion that artists spend all their time peering dreamily through the window into abstract worlds but that is not the case with Graham. The pressure has intensified when he has been drawn into the whirlpool of fundraising which can take years to accomplish and which he does not believe is part of his remit – but someone has to do it. Or when he is drawn into untangling the jungle called planning regulations when searching for a site for a sculpture. The borders and boundaries in his occupation, an unknown country, can become smudged – even before he has started work on the sculpture.

In America his approach to life would be called rugged individualism. In the UK this refusal to give in, his obsessive work ethic and his prudence in financial matters may be attributed to the fact that he is a Yorkshireman. Henry Moore, the acclaimed sculptor who taught for a time at the Royal College of Art, was the subject of a television documentary during which it became clear there were several threads running through his life which were familiar, though Graham would be the last person to put himself in the same league as Moore. Like Graham he was the son of a miner, from Castleford, and was highly proficient at drawing. He rejected the Victorian style of sculpting (Graham has also been unconventional in his approach to work) and his first work of art was based on an outcrop of rock which Moore and his father walked past on Sunday strolls during his childhood. (Familiar objects from the early years seem to become a compelling part of an artist's workload as they grow older. Over a period the images are refashioned, cut and elaborated upon and then fitted together in the imagination to form a remarkably diverse jigsaw on life.)

That documentary on Moore pointed out that the sculptor had been influenced by his childhood and by mining life, like Graham. A long-time friend with no apparent

'Only Just Married' … an example of his fascination with women who have strong characters. A woman and her nervous husband with suitcases are poised to find out who is the stronger sex – and the smart money is not on the man. The work was on show at an Austrian hotel for many years. *Ibbeson Collection*

'Redundant Fairy' … his take on the industrial upheaval which marked life in the UK in the late 1970s and early 1980s. It was shown at an exhibition sponsored by the Playboy Club of Munich and was sold to a client in America. *Freddy Neptune Limited*

Graham and his sister, Gail Arnold. *Ibbeson Family Archive*

The Raggy Lads, a blast from the past, with the Mayor at the unveiling of the Hucknall statue in Nottinghamshire. The men are the living embodiment of many of his influences sourced from the past. The 'lads' still maintain a way of life prevalent in working-class homes in the 1950s and can be seen drinking in various pubs in Barnsley town centre. *Ibbeson Collection*

Carol, Faye, Emma and Graham, having returned from London, are photographed on their first day in Barnsley. *Ibbeson Family Archive*

'Large Angel, Little Devil' … Graham served up another humorous work with this woman who has a halo.. or is it a dinner plate? *Freddy Neptune Limited*

'Maiden Voyage' … a woman taking her children into the great unknown. *Ibbeson Collection*

'Love and Carriage'. *Freddy Neptune Limited*

association with the North was asked why he thought Moore had been so successful. His genius was not mentioned, nor was the influence of parents, teachers or tutors. His reply was straightforward: 'It's because he was a Yorkshireman.' Could the same be said of Graham?

But that is not the complete picture. It's difficult to pinpoint the source of anybody's creativity and inventiveness. I have asked Graham on several occasions to identify the subconscious impulses, emotions and thoughts that have propelled him through life and enriched his talent but have not received a satisfactory answer. That probably goes for all artists, for brilliance is a gift, though people do try to define it. Genius has been described as 'a level of capability or achievement that exceeds the accomplishment of almost any other person in the same field' and as 'excellent work that is more than just originality'.

Other people would rely on the words of Sir Ian McGregor, a former chairman of the National Coal Board, who once said talent was 90 per cent perspiration and ten per cent inspiration. The American news magazine, *Time*, once attempted to analyse the qualities of Jonathan Franzen, now seen as a great American novelist, by burrowing through his emotions. The writer Lev Grossman said with Franzen even anger was a source of energy and creativity when he was at his lowest ebb. 'You take your inspiration where you find it, or where it finds you,' he wrote.

Inspiration has often found Graham.

Chapter 10

Time to Reflect

On approaching the age of sixty Graham started to take stock of his forty-year career. In an interview he recalled the stories which have peppered his life and then revaluated his work by looking at the words of the art critics and writers, spoke about his friends and their influences and answered a few questions before coming to the conclusion he would not have changed his life.

Humour has been inserted seamlessly into his life since childhood and he relishes telling stories about himself and his friends. Twice he has been on the point of unwittingly embarrassing Royalty. The Morecambe incident has been mentioned but there was an earlier one, in 1985. Graham was asked to prepare a work for Terminal 4 at Heathrow Airport. His faithful fibreglass chums, George and Eric, were brought in for service. George was depicted standing on a luggage truck with his brother Eric on his shoulders holding a placard which read: 'Welcome home, Mam'. The idea was that the lads had gone to the airport to welcome their mother. The authorities liked the idea – family and all that – but they probably thought the word 'Mam' would bewilder foreign visitors as well as a few of the hoity-toity brigade in the UK, so the man on the phone said they wanted the placard to read: 'Welcome to Britain'.

Graham said: 'They were paying so I obliged, even though the sentiment had changed. The sculpture was installed and just before the Royal opening I received a phone call. They liked how I had misspelt Britain, as if by a seven-year-old. The piece was for the arrival hall and the caller said the statue could cause some confusion – any visitors who were not bright would believe they were in another country. There was a pregnant pause but the confusion was down to me. I had spelt Britain incorrectly (Britian) and unintentionally. The lettering was altered before Princess Diana did the honours.'

Life became too hot to handle the day he was at the centre of a scene that could have appeared in a Laurel and Hardy sketch. Graham set himself on fire. While using a hot-air gun to soften and polish the wax on a plaque at home, he was distracted and a can of wax caught fire. Smoke billowed out of his carport, Carol thought next door's dustbins were on fire and Graham, in his burning plastic clogs, performed a dance which would have caused a cloudburst had he been a Red Indian medicine man.

'Welcome to Britain'. *Ibbeson Collection*

The Human Candle. *Barnsley Chronicle*

11.02.09   barnsleyindepend

ARTIST TURNS INTO A HUMAN CANDLE

BY JOHN THRELKELD

IT was like a scene out of a Les Dawson sketch. Graham Ibbeson was waxing a bronze plaque, 'Les Dawson the comedian' when he caught fire.

He was using a hot air gun to soften and polish the wax on the plaque when he was distracted and a tin of wax caught fire.

Clouds of smoke billowed out of his car port in Barnsley and Graham's plastic shoes caught fire.

"I was dancing around with my shoes on fire," he said. "My wife saw the smoke and thought next door's bins were on fire. I managed to kick the tin out of the way and out of danger; then I tried to wet a blanket to put out the flames."

Luckily a roofer doing work on the house saw him in distress.

He said: "As I was dancing I told him: 'I think I have got it under control' but he came across, realised what the situation was and said: 'You... haven't got it under control.'

"The man grabbed a fire extinguisher; the flames were put out and I had foam up to my knees. My feet were all right, my socks were singed and I threw the shoes into the dustbin. Then I went out and bought two fire extinguishers."

Graham joked: "I think the roofer thought that unless he helped out he would not get paid if the place burnt down."

n Graham's sculpture of Les Dawson was unveiled at St Anne's, Lancashire, on October 24.

Fireman: Sculptor Graham Ibbeson.   (S)

Mould making for the Cary Grant commission. *Ibbeson Collection*

146

A roofer working on the house gave him a blank look. 'I think I have got it under control,' Graham cried as his toes tingled and twinkled in their fiery dance. 'I do not think you have,' the roofer bawled back as he grabbed a fire extinguisher and put out the flames. Graham's feet were okay, the socks were singed but the shoes were ruined.

'I have always seen myself as a bit of a clown. I enjoy making people laugh, lifting spirits, because life can be grim. When I set my plastic clogs on fire I could feel Stan and Ollie's spirit running through my panic stricken feet. It did not matter that my pals and family read about it in the *Barnsley Chronicle*, it made me feel more human; their jokes and laughter were reward enough.'

Graham insists the viewers should wallow in the wonderful ridiculousness of his work. Humour is a kaleidoscope through which he sees the ever changing patterns and ironies of life. However, critics and writers have revealed other factors under the surface of his amusing work. Peter Murray, founding director of the Yorkshire Sculpture Park, wrote: 'Divertingly innocent, his sculpture demonstrates a penetrating perception. His sculpture, often witty in conception, is influenced by humorous events, popular imagery and images taken from comics and children's books. According to Ibbeson they are concerned with real people, believable characters with a past, present and future. It is all there: human frailty and misfortune; the fantastic and the surreal; the sinister and grotesque as well as the romantic… However, like the great comedians, Ibbeson is a serious artist who has worked hard to find the means of giving a tangible presence to his one liners. He also recognises the isolation and self effacement often referred to by other artists concerned with the sad world of humour. The laconic, wry humour of Ibbeson has given rise to some memorable sculptural imagery.'

The late Adrian Henri, the poet and painter, commenting on Graham's work at a Summer Show at the Serpentine Art Gallery in 1981, wrote: 'Ibbeson's skill can easily be missed in our enjoyment of the humour and charm of his subject matter. The work here is of two kinds, unified by a common theme: flight. 'Biggles', the 'Wrong Brothers' and others represent his continuing nostalgia for a 1930s comic-book world, in which Just William merges with Captain (W E) Johns' hero and Bonzo the Dog: a schoolboy Icarus with cardboard wings has sticking plaster on his knees, testimony to earlier attempts. Other figures, like the life-sized 'Redundant Fairy' have greater pathos: a post industrial Angel, beautiful, sad in her iron crown, one of Rossetti's ladies lost in Barnsley in the wrong century.'

Brian Elliott, author and historian, stated in 2006: 'No, I am not comparing Ibbeson to Michelangelo (I can hear Graham laughing in the background) but his creations mean more to me. They make me laugh. They make me think, and I must admit several of his mining creations make me cry. Isn't that what good art is all about? Graham's

Almost lifelike … Cary Grant statue, Bristol. *Ibbeson Collection*

Robin Hood and Little John. Robin was one of his daughter's ex-boyfriends and Little John was based on a builder from Barnsley. *Barnsley Chronicle*

devotion to capturing the spirit of the people appears in all his sculptures which is why they communicate so well with ordinary folk. His work is in many private collections and public museums around the world but many also serve as highly accessible public art sited in public places for all to enjoy.'

Some of the journalism has taken Graham by surprise. In a *Guardian* scribe's feature on the unveiling of the Cary Grant statue in Bristol he suggested Graham had a lot in common with Archie Leach (Grant's real name). 'They both worked hard at creating Cary Grant, at conjuring base matter into movie legend.' Graham was quoted as saying:

'Fishcake Jake' *Ibbeson Collection*   'North Sea Nippers'. *Ibbeson Collection*

'The thing about Grant was that he made everything look so easy. What people don't realise is that there was a lot of hard graft that went into that. It was the same with the sculpture. The way he stands there, he looks like he doesn't have a care in the world. But it was a pain in the arse to make.'

On occasions journalists have infuriated him. Celebrity Janet Street-Porter's comments touched a sensitive spot. In an acrimonious assault on public sculpture – she criticised both sculptors and local authorities – she described the Eric Morecambe and Laurel and Hardy statues as banal, a tag which Graham has dismissed with the conclusion she doesn't know what she is talking about. 'Janet Street-Porter can write what she wants but she rarely thinks before she writes.' The *Yorkshire Post* said she missed the point of his work 'and the innate skill and humour that pervades it'.

She says public art is what everyone thinks will give the community an identity. This idea has mushroomed since 'The Angel of the North' put Gateshead on the map, but in her opinion there was a danger that local councils would pollute the landscape with public art in the same way as electricity pylons have scarred the countryside.

Daughter Emma's statue. This wonderful life-like figure was produced to emphasise the theme that children 'should be seen and not heard'. It is now on view at the Northallerton (North Yorkshire) hospital. *Ibbeson Collection*

The mean looking 'Wrong Brothers' as opposed to the Wright Brothers, who were the first to fly in a machine that was heavier than air. The flat cap, the traditional emblem of Barnsley, gives the work the Ibbeson look. *The Yorkshire Sculpture Park*

In other parts of the globe the erection of statues has become an inane preoccupation. In La Gloria, eastern Mexico, there is one in memory of Edgar Hernandez, a small boy whose claim to fame was that he was the first patient to contract the H1N1 virus, while the town of Salem in America, where the seventeenth-century witch hunts took place, has been chosen as the site for a statue of Elizabeth Montgomery, star of TV's *Bewitched*, riding on a broomstick. 'It's an insult to what happened in 1692,' says a local resident.

Graham says this country has kept a level head and has not gone off into cloud cuckoo land. He believes the public's voice must be heard: 'Have I got it wrong or what? Shouldn't public art be for the public? Most of my public commissioned work originated from a proposal from the community and was selected in competition by a public vote. I pride myself on not being elitist; the opposite can be said of some of the so-called intellectuals, the art professionals who consider accessibility a crime against their minority. Maybe they are frightened that we may discover they have elevated themselves to a lofty position on the assumption that the populace is dumb, do not have an opinion or do not have the intellect or capability of judgment. Guidance is always needed but why should this elite, arrogant club dictate what goes on in our high street? They already control most of what goes in our public galleries.'

One of his pals, Chris Cooper (second left) and his band. Looking on are some of Graham's mute mates, the figures of WC Fields and Eric Presley. *Ibbeson Collection*

Newspapers have joined the debate. An evening newspaper in Lancashire has been firing a volley of insults against a statue depicting half an aqueduct at Preston. While having reservations about the monstrosity, the writer came out in support of Graham's work, pointing out that the Eric Morecambe figure is playful, amusing , greatly appealing and looks like the comedian. The writer added: 'It's great fun, people love it and it's brought some sunshine to the town that shares the great comedian's name.'

Surely that writer was correct. The critics have forgotten that a newspaper put a camera near the Eric Morecambe statue, after which some extraordinary scenes were recorded as families congregated, peered at the bronze figure and then tried to emulate the comedian's madcap stance by performing antics that would have surpassed the talents of a contortionist – all for the benefit of their Dads with cameras. The figure is hugely popular,

Comedian Norman Wisdom thought this little character was based on him. It was more likely to have been inspired by Graham's father-in law with a few touches plucked from the melting pot in the artist's imagination. *Ibbeson Collection*

Nicholas Treadwell, his agent, who has been exhibiting his work for forty years, and Graham and Carol, with a work of art, 'Mother Sucker'. It was sold that day. *Ibbeson Collection*

Landscape artist Ashley Jackson and Graham have exhibited their work at joint shows on a number of occasions. Both were brought up in Barnsley, a town not known for its connections with the art world, and both found that making their way in the early years was not easy. But the hard work has paid off. Ashley (left) Graham (centre) and Jack Brown, a Raggy Lad (right). *Chick Linsky*

His biggest achievement has been to make people laugh. This is 'The Great Escape', with the 'Grimethorpe Flyer', plus dog and the map which will enable them to get out of Barnsley. *Ibbeson Collection*

'The Gardener' … This was produced for the international garden festival at Stoke-on-Trent. *Ibbeson Collection*

a focal point for day trippers, and that's the ultimate benediction. There is nothing else to say save that there is a chance the next generation of visitors may not know who Eric Morecambe the comedian was, since fame is fleeting, but the statue will still draw them in simply because it's a national institution and an attraction in its own right.

Graham came up with some surprising views when reviewing his life. What was his biggest achievement?

'It has been ploughing my furrow while remaining an independent spirit. I am still riddled with self-doubt, and I always will be. I am my biggest critic. I have been slagged off by the best. However, art critics lack the imagination and creativity to compete with any artist's criticism of himself. Some of my greatest achievements have been sculptures that have provoked laughter. I have also been given the opportunity to produce portraits (public sculptures) of my comedy and industrial heroes.'

Any regrets?

'As I get older my biggest regret is that I should have said no to more people as well as to myself. I am now paying the price physically for not being strong enough and for not admitting defeat on some projects. On a personal note, I regret that Carol has never learnt to drive. I wanted a wife who would drive me to drink. It never happened.'

Would he do it all over again?

'I have enjoyed the challenge that has earned me this creative, privileged life. At times there is a weariness way above the physical and at other times an exhilaration that can only be obtained by being successful in bringing your original conceptions to life. I still have a lot more to say as a sculptor but I also know I just haven't got time to produce all I want to say. I used to have this fear that someone would find out that I was pretending to be a sculptor but then I realised I am one of a few who wasn't. The answer to the original question is: Yes.'

Is there anything that gives him a quirky sense of satisfaction?

'The local secondary modern school was harsh, but all the kids were in the same boat. Most of the fathers worked down the pit on low wages, their families were skint and living in council houses. I was taller and heavier than most of my classmates, but it didn't stop me getting bullied. On the contrary, I was a victim, a target. I won some and lost some. I was once standing in the playground and out of the blue this kid came up and karate chopped me in the mouth. Before I could retaliate properly I was hauled in front of the headmaster for starting the scuffle. The attack resulted in the loss of a tooth. I am knocking on sixty years of age and though I have had a false tooth, and now have a permanent bridge, every time I look in the mirror the gap in my smile reminds me of that day. The kid in question slicked his hair back with margarine (the Elvis look was still in during the early 1960s) and when the temperature increased his makeshift hair gel melted and he used to lick away the drips that ran down his face. I got my revenge later.'

What about the future? Graham will produce the statue to mark the life and times of Don Revie, the former manager of Leeds United FC, who helped to revolutionise football with his Revie plan in the 1950s when playing for Manchester City, and who made United into a trophy winning side in the 1960s and early 1970s. It will be located in the heart of the city. The project has involved working with and getting the approval of Revie's son, Duncan, and daughter, Kim. As part of a programme to involve the Yorkshire community in the project, small groups will be invited on a regular basis to visit him in his studio to watch the work in progress. Those invited will be schools, art colleges, Leeds United supporters' clubs, Chambers of Commerce, trade associations, community groups and the sponsors of the statue.

Over forty years he has met many people from all walks of life; there are several who have made a significant contribution to his life and who have not been mentioned in earlier chapters, Lee Winter, a pal at the Royal College in the 1970s, who played an important part in Graham's early years as a student; the last of his comic heroes, the late Norman Wisdom; Chris Cooper, a musician, and Ashley Jackson, the landscape painter.

Lee, assistant caretaker at the film school at the Royal College of Art, supplemented his income by cleaning the toilets. Like Graham, he had attended a secondary modern school, after which he fled to London from Scotland. Both helped out in the foundry in an evening when Professor Meadows was working there. It was obvious Lee wanted to get into foundry work full time and one day Graham knocked on the professor's office door and before Lee knew what was happening, he was bundled inside and the door closed. Professor Meadows saw the scuffle and thought they had been fighting. Lee emerged smiling from a brief and impromptu interview, an indication he was to be taken on. He became one of the best polishers of bronze Graham has ever known. More success followed and Lee was asked to run the foundry for Lynn Chadwick, the sculptor, in Gloucestershire, and eventually set up his own foundry back in Scotland, becoming a sculptor in his own right.

'One day Lee and I had been drinking at our Holborn pub. We were singing as we walked back to the tube station; I think I was giving a rendition of *On Ilkley Moor Bahrt Tat* when we were asked to stop because we were causing a nuisance. We told the man where to get off, but he turned out to be a plain-clothes policeman and we spent the night in the cells at Holborn. The following morning we appeared before the bench and I was fined for being drunk and disorderly. Much to my surprise the magistrate recognised Lee, who got double my fine as a fortnight earlier he had appeared in court charged with being drunk in charge of a push bike.'

Clumsy Boy David and the Death of Venus (an Italian-inspired piece with art historical references).
Freddy Neptune Limited

Graham met comedian Norman Wisdom at a Comic Heritage event in Rochdale organised to celebrate the life of Gracie Fields, the singer. Later they met again at one of Graham's exhibitions in London where Norman showed interest in a small sculpture of a drunk with a flat cap – he thought it was him. In the mid-1990s Comic Heritage asked if it could use copies of the maquette of Eric Morecambe as an award for achievement in its field, a kind of Oscar, and Norman was one of the recipients. After the exhibition, at which Norman asked questions about the 'Eric', Graham wrote to the comedian to ask whether he could do a small portrait of him – but did not get a reply for a time.

One day Carol answered the phone. 'It's Norman,' said the caller. 'Norman who?' Then it clicked it was the legendary comedian and Carol, blushing, handed over the receiver to Graham. Norman, who said he had an 'Ibbeson' taking pride of place on his piano, said he would love Graham to go ahead and fashion a portrait. Then the comedian went on to say he was an artist as well, having done some watercolours and pointed out that he drew the crowds wherever he went.

Graham asked him to suggest a pose. 'The pose?' asked Norman, to which Graham replied: 'Yes, the stance.' 'Oh,' said Norman, 'I thought you meant the jerry under the bed, the po.' Eventually Graham sent off the 'little Norman' and received a glowing thank you letter from his home in the Isle of Man and he has been thanked again on numerous occasions when they have met.

Most artists are loners, though Graham has a strong family around him and he has had the unusual knack of producing 'families' when creating his statues. Like other artists, he works alone. For instance, the American writer, Jonathan Franzen, works in a rented office that he has stripped of all distractions; his computer, an old model, is not connected to the internet. Graham works in splendid isolation in his workshop surrounded by his works and the paraphernalia of the artist. Both have evolved systems by which they have come to terms with their own creativity and the need to avoid human contact while working as artists.

Graham, however, has a kinsman in a musician, Chris, of Wakefield, who has played with many acclaimed guitarists. Graham said: 'There is intensity in making art that cannot be shared. You can do demonstrations and workshops to show the process but the creation of a work of art is a solitary activity. The outcome is so delicately balanced between success and failure that distraction will bring about its demise. On the social scene artists have a tendency to avoid each other like the plague since the intensity and passions of the job bubble to the surface and bring conflict. The one person with whom I feel comfortable discussing my creative ideas and my artistic problems is the musician Chris Cooper. We share the burden of trying to find solutions to creative problems through discussion. It all sounds very pretentious. More often than not the spirit of the debate usually falls apart on the approach of 'last orders' and then becomes a deep and meaningless conversation.'

Ashley Jackson, who was brought up in Barnsley, and who specialises in moorland scenes, is both a colleague and friend. They have staged several two-man exhibitions throughout the UK and at corporate venues in London sponsored by the Yorkshire/ Clydesdale Bank. 'On the surface our works and personalities seem to be at odds. Ashley is flamboyant and easy with an audience, I am a little reticent, and I do what I have to do and then take a back seat. Ashley's paintings are dark and moody, my sculpture and drawings are mostly light and optimistic, and instil a sense of fun. But we have more similarities than differences.'

Graham says the funniest people he has met have not been celebrities but friends and characters in the street. His friend and agent is Nicholas Treadwell, who lives in a converted jailhouse in Austria. He's seventy-three and dyes his hair pink to make people smile and to attract attention, though he does not get the latter in Barnsley, a typical hard town where they have seen it all before. 'I was not embarrassed on one occasion when he asked me to go round the charity shops in Barnsley looking for a disco dress for him for an event. The shopkeepers loved the challenge and the laughter could be heard down the street.'

Nicholas said: 'It's not easy to explain our relationship. Firstly it has been going on for thirty-three years and is now as strong as ever. He is the artist and I am the agent in our partnership and of course there has always been a business element between us, with the lows and highs that are part of the game at the level we play at. On balance this aspect of our relationship has remained consistent and commercially effective, with some particularly successful moments from time to time over the years.

'These factors alone make our thirty-three years of working together quite extraordinary. However, it is the substance and warmth of our ever blossoming friendship which I appreciate. It is as surprising as it is important to me. Graham is a down-to-earth naturally funny man, both in his art and in his life. One way or another both he and his creative work have kept me laughing throughout our time together. Since coming to live in Austria, I have taken to spending a night or two at Graham and Carol's home on my whistle-stop trips collecting art in England.

'They both make me welcome and naturally a pub crawl around Barnsley is an accepted part of my visit. Graham teases me that the pub crawl mission is to find me a suitably strong and sexy Barnsley lass to support me and my gallery well into my dotage. Of course I do not get close to any such dalliance but it is all part of our evening's good natured banter. Both Graham and I are hard workers, persistent survivors and loyal,

Family group (left to right, front): Jordan (grandson), Poppy (granddaughter), Graham and Carol, Mia (baby granddaughter); (back): James (Emma's partner), Emma (daughter), Faye (daughter), Max (son) and Debbie (daughter-in-law). *Ibbeson Family Archive*

with recognition and respect for each other's abilities. Generally we are as different as the proverbial chalk and cheese, but somehow we connect. I like Graham very much and I am always glad to see him and thoroughly enjoy spending time with him.

'Making funny sculptures every day of your life is a very serious business, but considering his life's works to date I can without doubt say that Graham has made some of the world's funniest sculpture classics. His sculptural heroes and heroines have been his wonderful cleaning ladies, his plumbers, his lost scouts, the naughty children of his mining family background; imperfect but lovable – hopefully like most of us.'

He brought sunshine into people's lives … Eric Morecambe, one of the nation's iconic statues, rounds off the book. *Ibbeson Collection*

One of the local characters is the son of Graham's grandfather's best mate, Frank Hardman, junior, who worked at Grimethorpe Colliery where he carried on his father's tradition of making 'em laugh. Stories about these characters become part of village folklore and are told in pubs and on street corners until a new generation of funny men, unheralded save in their own neighbourhoods, come along with their own yarns. Some stories are true, others are fables. Frank junior's is a true story and dates from the days of the pits.

The National Coal Board (British Coal) had changed the rules on holidays so workers had a choice of dates (before that pits closed for a week or fortnight in August). His mates had booked two weeks as usual including Barnsley Feast Week, the town's traditional holiday break. Frank had gone for two other weeks, the first of which he spent sat in a deck chair on the roof of the pit canteen dressed in a brightly coloured shirt and straw hat. He roared with laughter as his workmates went to work.

Graham said he is the stuff of legends. Mick Wilson, who became a professional artist, worked at the same pit and knew Frank. While standing at the bus stop, and praying that the pit bus ('pit paddy') would arrive before Frank and his motor-bike and sidecar, Mick on occasions shivered in chill anticipation. 'There would be a terrifying trip from Cudworth to Grimethorpe with Frank singing his head off and Mick screaming in the side car.'

Graham's life has been interwoven with this kind of story. When the pressure is on and the clamour is overwhelming he sits back and muses over those stories and his forty-year career. He thinks of the embarrassing incidents like the crayon up the nose and the distant world of Frank Hardman, senior, and the homely New Year's Eve party all those years ago, the best party the world had ever known.

He also thinks of his families who are embedded in his life. As well as his biological family, he has accumulated other 'families' such as the gnomes who were ensconced in a cottage at college, the Vikings and their children at York and his statues scattered around the UK and on the continent. He must have the most sublime, expensive and unusual family album in the world. Whereas most families have pages full of photographs, his collection is cast in bronze or fibre glass, a perceptive record of his family's ageing process. Instead of browsing among photographs he can stroll one hundred yards down the road to view the miners' sculptures which are so proudly and movingly frozen in time. The figures, an elegy to mining families, seem to radiate emotion and sorrow and each time you take a close look you see something new in the faces.

Yet the statues, once seen as innovative and hauntingly reminiscent of another age, are now so integrated into the townscape that they barely elicit a glance from passing motorists or pedestrians. In a way they are like the nearby National Union of

Mineworkers offices. In the 1970s and 1980s the building, once dubbed 'King Arthur's (Scargill's) Castle' by a journalist, was never off the television screens and journalists spent hours in the entrance hall waiting for important union council meetings to end. In those days the union appeared to wield extraordinary power and miners were described as the storm troopers of the trade union movement, the battle hardened men who spearheaded trade union campaigns. Today the union, having been bludgeoned into submission by the 1984 strike and the subsequent pit closure programme, is a shadow of its former self and has a membership of several thousand rather than the one million of nearly 100 years ago. The offices, like the statues, are no longer the centre of attention and passers-by rarely look at the ornate and fussy Victorian building which appears to be out of place in an area where glass and concrete blocks are being built (the college and nearby Westgate Plaza).

But, unlike the 'castle', the statues are not intrusive and sit quietly and comfortably near the road junction, gentle reminders of an industrial age that degraded and brutalised man. They will be there long after the offices have closed.

Imagine Graham touring the UK in search of his wife and children. He would see their faces, albeit 'photographed' at different ages, in Perth, Jarrow, Rugby, South Yorkshire and in Sherwood Forest (where Carol is Maid Marian, an ex-boyfriend of Faye's is Robin and a builder from Barnsley is Little John). There is a likeness to his father, who was used as a model for one of the miners at Hucknall and he knows his late father-in-law, Charlie, whose personality and features are immortalised in fibreglass, and who was always smiling in Ripley, has a permanent smile somewhere on the continent.

Northampton would be included in his itinerary should he wish to be reminded of himself and his sister when they were children, a perceptive portrait which captures the freedom, movement and joy of uninhibited play. Further south, at the Museum of Childhood in Bethnal Green in London, both daughters have been featured there in the past, though Emma's figure is now at a hospital in Northallerton. (Bethnal Green is the museum which commissioned his model of 'Just William' which personifies all the mischievous qualities of boyhood.)

As a final thought on this topic, one can imagine a rail company producing tourist maps and booklets with montages of attractions in each town or city including pictures or sketches of his sculptures and wall reliefs. Graham says: 'The statues will be there after everyone else has gone.'

And despite setbacks in his forty-year career he can still dream. He had dreams and aspirations when he was a student and a young sculptor, though he never anticipated reaching such an exalted peak as having the privilege of working on the comedians whose humour and personalities have helped to mould his career. One statue stands above all others, however. It was unveiled on a special day, an important episode in his life. In the reverie he's strolling breezily on the gaily decked-out Morecambe seafront with families beginning to gather for the arrival of Her Majesty the Queen. The sun is glinting on the sea, he's heading towards 'Eric' and, this time around, he hasn't a care in the world.

No mallet, no green splurge, no worries.

Appendix 1

Biographical Details

1951	Born 13 August 1951
1962–66	Cudworth Secondary Modern School, Barnsley
1966-67	Apprentice Electrician, NCB Workshops, Shafton, Barnsley
1967-68	Barnsley School of Art
1968-71	Thornton's Sweets (Belper)
	Butterley Steel Company (Ripley)
1969	Married Carol Greenwood
1970	Daughter, Faye born
1971-72	Chesterfield School of Art
1972-73	Leicester Polytechnic
1973-75	Trent Polytechnic (Nottingham)
1974	Daughter, Emma born
1975	BA(Hons) Fine Art (1st Class)
1975-78	Royal College of Art (London)
1978	Madame Tussaud's Award for Figurative Art
1978	MA (R.C.A.) Sculpture
1978-81	Taught part-time, Leeds Polytechnic (Fine Art Department)
1980-81	Taught part-time Manchester Polytechnic (Sculpture Department)
1983	Son, Max born

Self Employed. *Ibbeson Collection*

Appendix 2

Exhibitions & Commissions

1. SOLO EXHIBITIONS, 1975-2010

1975	Nottingham Castle Museum & Art Gallery
1975	Bedworth Arts Centre
1983	Towner Art Gallery, Eastbourne
1983	Aberystwyth Arts Centre
1984	Middlesbrough Art Gallery
1987	Art 17, Basel (Switzerland)
1988	Doncaster Museum & Art Gallery
1989	Rufford Park, Nottingham
1990	Yorkshire Sculpture Park (Wakefield)
1991	Marcus & Marcus Gallery, Amsterdam
1991	Treadwell's Art Mill, Bradford
1992	Glynn Vivian Art Gallery, Swansea
1993	Midsummer Gallery, Milton Keynes

Angel Fish. *Ibbeson Collection*

1994	Doncaster Museum & Art Gallery
1994	Elizabethan Gallery, Wakefield
1995	Durham Museum & Art Gallery
1996	Rotherham Art Gallery
1996	Rufford Orangery, near Nottingham
1998	Derby City Art Gallery
1998	Cox's Yard, Stratford-upon-Avon
1999	The Ashbourne Gallery
2001	Die Station Gallery, Neufelden (Austria)
2006	Nicholas Treadwell Gallery, Aigen (Austria)
2006	Fredmansky Gallery, Graz (Austria)
2009	3 Albion Place, Leeds
2009	Tregoning Fine Art, Derby
2011	Hive Gallery, Elsecar, Barnsley

13 Amp Confused. *Ibbeson Collection*

2. SELECTED GROUP EXHIBITIONS, 1977-2010

1980	Women 1980 (Die Insel Gallery, Munich)
1981	Summer Show 2 (Serpentine Art Gallery, London)
	Superhumanism (Ostermaln Gallery, Stockholm)
1984	Attitudes '84 (Yorkshire Sculpture Park)
	Superhumanism (Arnold Katzen Gallery, New York)
1986	Bretton Menagarie (Yorkshire Sculpture Park)

International Garden Festivals:

1984	Liverpool
1986	Stoke-on-Trent
1988	Glasgow
1992	Ebbw Vale
2007	From Yorkshire with Love (with Ashley Jackson), sponsored by Clydesdale Bank, corporate venues in Knightsbridge, London /Canary Wharf, London/ Richmond, Surrey

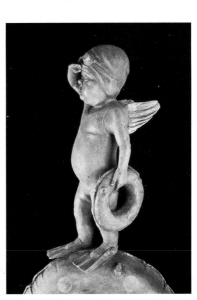

Shown with the Nicholas Treadwell Gallery since 1977 at international venues in Europe, USA and Asia

Shown with the Tregoning Gallery since 1998

Life Guardian. *Freddy Neptune Limited*

3. SELECTED GALLERIES (Mixed Exhibitions), 1977-2010
Taraman Gallery (London)
Mansion House (Doncaster)
Gallery Yolanda (Chicago)
Studio 53 (New York)
Grand Palais (Paris)
Cooper Art Gallery (Barnsley)
Rugby Museum & Art Gallery
Leeds City Art Gallery
Bethnal Green Museum of Childhood (London)

Look North. *Ibbeson Collection*

4. WORKS IN MANY PUBLIC and PRIVATE COLLECTIONS, including:
The British Council
Victoria & Albert Museum (Bethnal Green Museum of
    Childhood)
Nottinghamshire County Council
Canadian Arts Council
South Tees NHS
Barnsley MBC
Prudential Insurance (London)
Bristol City Art Gallery & Museum
Leeds City Art Gallery (Arthur Aaron Maquette)
Yorkshire County Cricket Ground (Headingley, Leeds)

The Losers. *Freddy Neptune Ltd*

5. COMMISSIONS (Various):
Commonwealth Institute (London)
London Symphony Orchestra
York Archaeological Trust
Victoria & Albert Museum (London)
British Airport Authority
KFW Bank (Dusseldorf)
MEXX (Amsterdam)
Middlesbrough MBC
Guardian Royal Assurance
Wakefield MDC

Milk Dictator. *Freddy Neptune Ltd*

Dover District Council
Nottingham County Council
Eurotunnel (Folkestone)
Center Parcs
Barnsley MBC
Harvey Nichols (London)

Bronze Public Commissions
NORTHAMPTON SCULPTURE 1986
(4 metre high bronze on Westmorland Slate)

THOMAS CHIPPENDALE (Otley, Yorkshire) 1987
(7ft 6ins bronze on Yorkstone)

THE JIM MACFARLANE MEMORIAL SCULPTURE
(Conisbrough, Doncaster, 1987)
(2 life-size bronze figures)

SCALES OF JUSTICE (Middlesbrough) 1990
(3 life-size figures on Yorkstone)

MINERS' MEMORIAL (Barnsley, Yorkshire) 1992
(3 life-size figures on granite)

A WIFE ON THE OCEAN WAVES (Cardiff) 1993
(Bronze life-size family in a bronze bath)

THE FAIR MAID OF PERTH (Perth, Scotland) 1995
(Life-size bronze figure)

WILLIAM WEBB ELLIS (Rugby) 1996
(8ft bronze on Yorkstone)

KATE (Chesterfield) 1997
(Life-size bronze)

'Drunk.' *Freddy Neptune Limited*

Yarling Baby. *Freddy Neptune Ltd*

RUN RUN RUNAWAY (Chesterfield) 1998
(2 metre high bronze)

TIMOTHY HACKWORTH (Shildon, Co Durham) 1998
(Life-size bronze on Yorkstone)

ERIC MORECAMBE (Morecambe, Lancs) 1999
(A little above life-size figure in bronze)

THE LEEDS MILLENNIUM SCULPTURE 2001
(5 life-size bronze figures/5 metre high Sculpture)

THE SPIRIT OF JARROW (Jarrow, Tyneside) 2001
(5 life-size bronze figures on stainless steel)

CARY GRANT (Bristol) 2001
(Life-size bronze)

REDCAR PANELS (Redcar, Cleveland) 2002
(Three 7 mtr long by 3.5mtr wide panels in stainless steel
and bronze

PETER ROBINSON (Castlereagh Town Hall) 2003
(Life-size bronze portrait)

HUCKNALL MINERS' MEMORIAL 2005
(Hucknall, Nottingham)
(Twice life-size miner on 12ft miners lamp in bronze)

SOUTH KIRKBY MINER (For South Kirkby &
Moorthorpe Town Council) 2004–5
(Life-size bronze miner)

WILLIAM WEBB ELLIS (for Menton, France) 2008
(4ft bronze figure commissioned as part of the 2008 Rugby
World Cup)

Hucknall unveiling event. *Ibbeson Collection*

Dickie Bird unveiling. *Brian Elliott*

Fred at the Foundry. *Ibbeson Collection*

BENNY HILL (for Southampton) 2007
(Life-figure in bronze) Work in progress

LES DAWSON (for Lytham St Annes) 2008
(Over life-size figure in bronze)

LAUREL & HARDY (for Ulverston, Cumbria) 2009
(Life-size bronze figures)

HAROLD (DICKIE) BIRD (for Barnsley) 2009
(Over life-size bronze figure)

FRED TRUEMAN (for Skipton) 2009
(Over life-size figure in bronze)

KELLINGLEY MINERS' MEMORIAL (Pontefract, 2010)
(Life-size bronze figure in relief)

FORTHCOMING:

DAVID WHITFIELD (for Hull)
(Life-size figure in bronze)

DON REVIE (for Leeds)
(7ft figure in bronze)

Kellingley Miners' Memorial.
Ibbeson Collection

Studio life. *Ibbeson Collection*

Modelling Tom Finney.
Ibbeson Collection

Index